foolproof Crazy-Quilt Projects

Jennifer Clouston

10 PROJECTS

Seam-by-Seam Stitch Maps

Stitch Dictionary

Full-Size Patterns

C&T PUBLISHING

Text copyright © 2016 by Jennifer Clouston

Photography and artwork copyright © 2016 by C&T Publishing, Inc.

Publisher: Amy Marson

Creative Director: Gailen Runge

Art Director: Kristy Zacharias

Editor: Liz Aneloski and Joanna Burgarino

Technical Editors: Priscilla Read and Debbie Rodgers

Cover/Book Designer: April Mostek

Production Coordinators: Jenny Davis and Freesia Pearson Blizard

Production Editor: Joanna Burgarino

Illustrator: Mary E. Flynn

Photo Assistant: Mary Peyton Peppo

Instructional photography by Diane Pedersen, unless otherwise noted

Published by C&T Publishing, Inc., P.O. Box 1456, Lafayette, CA 94549

Library of Congress Cataloging-in-Publication Data

Clouston, Jennifer, 1959- author.

Foolproof crazy-quilt projects : 10 projects, seam-by-seam stitch maps, stitch dictionary, full-size patterns / Jennifer Clouston.

pages cm

ISBN 978-1-61745-132-4 (soft cover)

1. Crazy quilts. 2. Patchwork--Patterns. 3. Quilting--Patterns. I. Title.

TT835.C5994 2016

746.46'041--dc23

2015027787

Printed in China

10 9 8 7 6 5 4 3 2 1

Dedication

To the kindred spirits out there who find peace, enjoyment,

and a sense of fulfillment in the simple act of attaching

a single bead, finding the perfect thread, and creating

sumptuous seam treatments

Acknowledgments

This book would not have been possible without the immeasurable contribution of my husband, Vaughn. His practical intuitiveness, technical proficiency, and unrelenting commitment to a deadline are the reasons you are able to hold this book in your hands.

His engineering background has twice proved useful in my career as a crazy-quilt maker—with this book and previously in his contribution on my first book, *Foolproof Crazy Quilting*. He manages to decipher the ideas and shapes in my head and translate them into patterns on paper that anyone who has never even picked up a needle before can use to create wonderful, crazy patterns.

I am also grateful to the many people who have come together to make this book happen.

To Liz and the talented team at C&T Publishing, thank you.

To my friend and neighbor Jane, who donned many hats during my book-writing process—therapist, patient listener, quality controller, and a calming influence. Thank you.

To my children, Gareth and Ainslie, thank you for replying to my desperate calls for help regarding color choice and design.

Lastly, to my students, who encourage, motivate, and stimulate me. You asked the question: "Have you started your next book?" My answer is, "Yes, I have, and here it is."

Contents

Projects

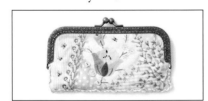

Stitch Dictionary

Introduction

"Have nothing in your house that you do not find useful or believe to be beautiful." —*William Morris*

Taking the advice from Mr. Morris, we can transform our useful into beautiful and thereby have the best of both worlds: a tablet purse becomes an embroidered masterpiece and a functional tea cozy can double as an eye-catching centerpiece on our table.

Welcome to a world of crazy quilting, where any type of fabric goes: bright and bold, subdued Japanese cottons, "upcycled" wool, pretty ginghams, and vintage doilies.

Each project comes with detailed assembly instructions and easy-to-follow stitch maps. The pullout pattern sheets include full-size patterns for each project.

The comprehensive stitch dictionary includes silk ribbon and basic embroidery, beading, and embellishing stitches.

Whether you are a new crazy quilter or an experienced crazy quilter looking for smaller projects to go "crazy" on, I am sure you will find something to inspire you.

China flower pincushion

Tea Cozy and Tablet Purse

Basic Sewing Requirements and Foundation Piecing

Basic Sewing Requirements

Basic sewing requirements

- Sewing machine and neutral thread
- Rotary cutter, mat, and board
- Embroidery scissors
- Pins
- Ruler
- Iron and ironing board
- Thread Heaven thread conditioner
- Appliqué glue
- Glue stick
- Metal spatula
- Small hair styling flat iron and silicon mat

Tip A recycled, vintage candleholder can be transformed into a handy sewing caddy.

Tips

- A small hair iron is the perfect tool to rid silk ribbon of any creases and to tame those unruly rayon embroidery threads. Use it with a silicon mat (oven mitt).

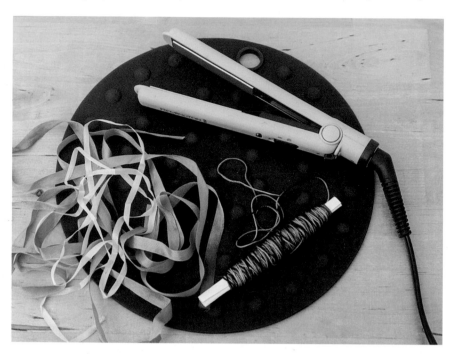

- A rounded metal icing spatula is a handy tool to have in your sewing box. It assists in creating smooth seams without the danger of pushing through the fabric. Keep the spatula between the layers when pressing the edges.

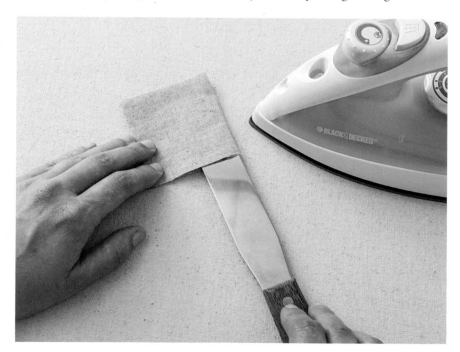

Foundation Piecing Requirements

- Foundation fabric
- Interesting fabrics
- Lightweight fusible fleece (I use Vilene H630 by Pellon.)
- Sewing machine and neutral thread
- Rotary cutter, mat, and board
- Embroidery scissors
- Freezer paper
- Pins
- Hera marker or marking pencil
- Ruler
- Iron and ironing board

Here are a few things to remember before beginning:

- Most, if not all, projects featured in this book are utility items; they were designed to be used frequently. The choice of fabrics is, therefore, very important. "Fancy" fabrics such as embossed velvets, satins, and antique fabrics do not stand up to the rigors of frequent handling and washing. Select from the wide range of cotton and silk fabrics to create your crazy projects.

- Crazy quilting is all about the embroidery and embellishing. Take the time to select fabrics that will showcase your seam treatments. Limit the amount of overly busy, fussy fabrics, because the embroidery will struggle to be seen.

- All the projects featured in this book require a foundation fabric. My foundation fabric of choice is a prewashed calico or quilter's muslin. There are many alternatives to muslin, but it is helpful to remember that a fabric with a low thread count is less damaging to the delicate fibers of the embroidery threads and silk ribbons as they pass through the fabric.

The maker of this antique quilt used a variety of foundation fabrics.

- Most projects featured in this book are pieced using the foundation method. There are many methods for piecing a crazy quilt. This is my least favorite stage of the crazy-quilting process, so I like to get it done as simply and quickly as I can. I find the foundation method to be the most accurate; it also allows for the fussy cutting of fabrics, if the need arises. The angular lines created by this method are conducive to seam treatments that may be heavily embroidered and embellished while still retaining the "shape" of the crazy pieces, which I prefer.

Foundation Piecing Method

> **NOTE**
>
> It is important to note that a generous ½″ seam allowance is needed in this method of piecing.

1. Trace the project design on the matte side of freezer paper. Number all the shapes.

2. Cut out the shapes from freezer paper; these shapes are now your templates.

3. Center and trace the project design and numbering onto the foundation fabric.

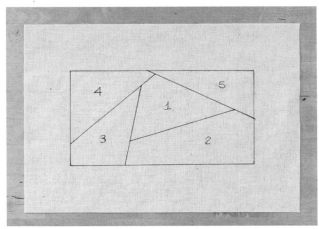

Trace project design on foundation fabric.

4. Stitch along the outer perimeter line of the marked project shape.

5. Select the fabrics.

6. Place the shiny side of the freezer paper on the right side of the fabric; press. Freezer paper is slightly transparent, so you can easily fussy cut your fabric.

Place freezer paper template on right side of fabric.

7. Cut out the shapes, adding a ½″ seam allowance.

8. Place the foundation fabric marked side up. Lay Piece 1 over Area 1 on the foundation fabric; the fabric should cover the perimeter lines of Area 1. Remove the freezer paper (it can be used many times).

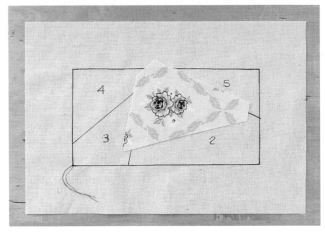

Place Piece 1 over Area 1.

9. Lay Piece 2 right side down on Shape 1. Make sure that when it is stitched, flipped, and pressed, the fabric covers the perimeter lines of Area 2 on the foundation fabric.

10. Place the ruler on the adjoining line between Pieces 1 and 2—lift the fabric slightly until the pencil line is visible. Align the ruler on this line and score the fabric with a Hera marker (or pencil). This is now your stitching line.

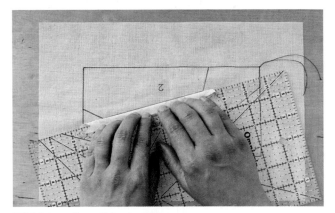

Lift fabric until pencil line is visible

11. Pin and stitch ½″ past the neighboring lines.

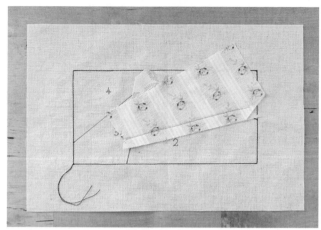

Pin and stitch.

12. Flip over Shape 2 and press well. It is very important to keep your work flat during this stage.

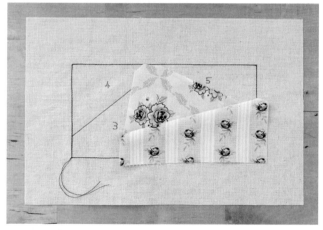

Flip and press.

13. Repeat Steps 8–12, working in numerical order, until the project design is complete.

14. Press well.

Tip I suggest that you use an appliqué mat or a sheet of baking paper while pressing to prevent the fabrics from scorching.

15. Place the project design wrong side up and sew on the perimeter line of the project shape (the line sewn at Step 7).

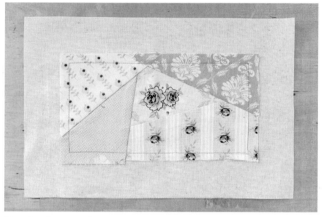

Completed project design

16. Fuse the fleece to the wrong side of the foundation fabric.

Tablet Purse

Finished size: 9½″ × 11″

A tablet purse, embellished and embroidered, makes for a very glamorous accessory.

FABRIC AND SUPPLIES

- Assorted fabric scraps at least 5″ × 8″
- 2 pieces of foundation fabric 13″ × 14″
- 2 pieces of lining fabric 11″ × 12″
- 2 pieces of lightweight fusible fleece 11″ × 12″ (I use Vilene H630 by Pellon.)
- 1 piece of backing fabric 11″ × 12″
- 1 rectangular purse frame 3½″ × 9½″

NEEDLES AND THREADS

- Milliners #03 needle for

  Perle cotton #8 and #12 thread

  Embroidery floss
- Milliners #09 needle for

  Nymo beading thread
- Chenille #22 needle for

  2mm, 4mm, 7mm, and 13mm silk ribbons

  Silk perle #8 and #12 thread

  Rayon ribbon floss

  Velvet thread

EMBELLISHMENTS

- 7mm silk ribbon for outer trim of completed tablet purse
- Small sequins
- Seed beads
- Selection of assorted beads for back

Fabrics, needles, and frame accessories

Construction

Pattern includes ¼″ seam allowance.

Making the Front Panel

Use Pattern 1 (pullout page P2) for the front panel.

1. Follow the foundation piecing method (page 10) to complete the front panel.

2. Follow the stitch maps (pages 14–16) to complete the seam treatments.

3. Trim the completed front panel on the cutting line.

Stitch Maps

SEAM TREATMENT A

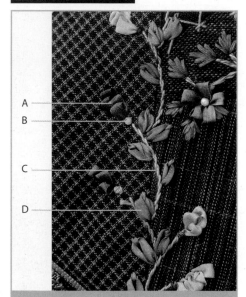

A. Plume stitch (page 88)
• 4mm silk ribbon

B. Stab stitch (page 91)
• 4mm silk ribbon

C. Stem stitch (page 92)
• Perle cotton #8 thread

D. Lazy daisy stitch (page 87)
• 4mm silk ribbon

SEAM TREATMENT B

A. Stab stitch (page 91)
• Silk perle #8 thread

B. Knotted fly stitch (page 86)
• 4mm silk ribbon

C. Lazy daisy stitch (page 87)
• 4mm silk ribbon

D. Stem stitch (page 92)
• Silk perle #8 thread

E. Herringbone stitch (page 86)
• Perle cotton #8 thread

SEAM TREATMENT C

A. Stab stitch leaf (page 92)
• Rayon ribbon floss

B. Loop stitch and flower (page 88)
• 4mm silk ribbon

C. Stem stitch (page 92)
• 2mm silk ribbon

D. Stab stitch (page 91)
• 2mm silk ribbon

SEAM TREATMENT D

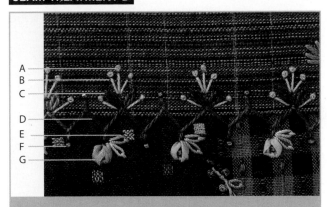

A. Colonial knot (page 82)
  • Perle cotton #8 thread

B. Stab stitch (page 91)

Perle cotton #8 thread

C. Lazy daisy stitch (page 87)
  • Perle cotton #8 thread

D. Cretan stitch (page 83)
  • Perle cotton #8 thread

E. Lazy daisy stitch (page 87)
  • Perle cotton #8 thread

F. Single-bead stitch (page 91)
  • Nymo beading thread

G. Lazy daisy stitch (page 87)
  • 4mm silk ribbon

SEAM TREATMENT E

A. Padded stab stitch (page 88)
  • 4mm silk ribbon

B. Twisted chain stitch (page 93)
  • Silk perle #8 thread

C. Lazy daisy stitch with bead (page 87)
  • Perle cotton #12 thread

D. Stab stitch (page 91)
  • Perle cotton #12 thread

SEAM TREATMENT F

A. Fly stitch leaf (page 85)
  • Silk perle #8 thread

B. Beaded/couched sequin (page 81)
  • Nymo beading thread

C. Zigzag chain stitch (page 94)
  • Perle cotton #8 thread

D. Colonial knot (page 82)
  • Perle cotton #8 thread

SEAM TREATMENT G

A. Stab stitch (page 91)
  • Silk perle #8 thread

B. Lazy daisy stitch (page 87)
  • Silk perle #8 thread

C. Colonial knot (page 82)
  • Silk perle #8 thread

D. Stem stitch with beads (page 93)
  • Silk perle #12 thread

SEAM TREATMENT H

A. Free-form flower with beaded center (page 86)
  • 13mm silk ribbon

B. Colonial knot (page 82)
  • 7mm silk ribbon

C. Ruched rose (page 90)
  • 7mm silk ribbon

D. Stab stitch (page 91)
  • 2mm silk ribbon

E. Ribbon stitch (page 89)
  • 4mm silk ribbon

F. Fishbone stitch (page 84)
  • Velvet thread

SEAM TREATMENT I

A. Lazy daisy stitch (page 87)
  • 4mm silk ribbon

B. Stem stitch (page 92)
  • Perle cotton #8 thread

C. Fishbone stitch (page 84)
  • 4mm silk ribbon

SEAM TREATMENT J

A. Lazy daisy stitch (page 87)
  • 4mm silk ribbon

B. Ribbon stitch (page 89)
  • 4mm silk ribbon

C. Feather stitch (page 84)
  • Perle cotton #8 thread

D. Beaded/couched sequin (page 81)
  • Nymo beading thread

E. Stab stitch (page 91)
  • A single strand of embroidery floss

F. Stab stitch (page 91)
  • A single strand of embroidery floss

Making the Back Panel

Use Pattern 1 (pullout page P2) for the back panel.

1. Trace the perimeter lines of Pattern 1 onto the right side of the backing fabric.

2. Fuse the fleece to the wrong side of the backing fabric.

3. Use a Hera marker to mark diagonal lines 2″ apart on the right side of the fabric.

4. Using perle cotton #12 thread or 3 strands of embroidery floss, hand quilt a running stitch along the marked lines. After every 2 stitches, pick up a bead to add texture.

5. Trim the completed back panel on the cutting line.

Bead to add texture

Adding the Lining

1. Trace the perimeter lines of the front panel onto the wrong sides of 2 pieces of lining fabric. Mark the 2 *'s on the fabric.

2. Put the front panel on a lining piece with rights sides together. Sew the top edge from * to *.

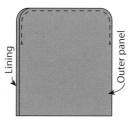

Sew top edge.

3. Repeat Steps 1 and 2 for the quilted back panel and the other piece of lining fabric.

Assembly

1. Pin only the lining panels, right sides together, and sew around the extended side seams of the *lining fabric only* from * to *, leaving a 4″ opening at the bottom of the lining fabrics for turning.

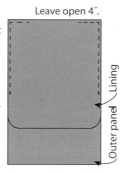

Sew around extended side seams.

2. Pin the front and side panels together and sew around the side seams from * to *.

Sew around side seams.

3. Gently turn the purse right side out through the opening. Use a spatula to gently push out the stitched seams; press lightly. Slipstitch the opening closed.

4. Open the purse frame and push the fabric into the frame.

5. Using 2 strands of perle cotton #8 thread and a milliners needle, stitch the purse to the frame, starting at the center and working outward, using a running stitch to go in and out of the holes in the frame.

6. Complete the border trim using a 7mm silk ribbon to make a ruched silk ribbon garland (page 90).

Sewing Pouch

Finished size: 5″ × 10″

A bright and funky sewing pouch

FABRIC AND SUPPLIES

- Small scraps at least 5˝ square for the crazy design

- 1 piece of foundation fabric 9˝ × 13˝

- 2 pieces of lining fabric each 9˝ x13˝

- 1 piece of backing fabric 9˝ × 13˝

- 2 pieces of lightweight fusible fleece 9˝ × 13˝ (I use Vilene H630 by Pellon.)

- 1˝ wide twill tape 120˝ (Or you can use binding.)

NEEDLES AND THREADS

- Milliners #03 needle for

  Perle cotton #8 thread

- Chenille #22 needle for

  4mm and 7mm silk ribbon

Fabrics, needles, threads, and tape

Construction

Pattern includes ¼˝ seam allowance.

Making the Front Panel

Use Pattern 2 (pullout page P3) for the front panel.

1. Follow the foundation piecing method (page 10) to complete the front panel.

2. Follow the stitch maps (pages 20–22) to complete the seam treatments.

3. Trim the completed front panel on the cutting line.

Stitch Maps

PIECE 1

A. Colonial knot (page 82)
- Perle cotton #8 thread

B. Lazy daisy stitch (page 87)
- 4mm silk ribbon

C. Lazy daisy stitch flower (page 87)
- 7mm silk ribbon

D. Twisted chain stitch (page 93)
- Perle cotton #8 thread

SEAM TREATMENT A

A. Lazy daisy stitch (page 87)
- Perle cotton #8 thread

B. Stab stitch (page 91)
- Perle cotton #8 thread

C. Herringbone stitch (page 86)
- Perle cotton #8 thread

D. Colonial knot (page 82)
- Perle cotton #8 thread

E. Stab stitch (page 92)
- Perle cotton #8 thread

F. Colonial knot (page 82)
- Perle cotton #8 thread

SEAM TREATMENT B

A. Lazy daisy stitch (page 87)
- Perle cotton #8 thread

B. Colonial knot (page 82)
- Perle cotton #8 thread

C. Stab stitch (page 91)
- Perle cotton #8 thread

SEAM TREATMENT C

A   —
B   —

A. Fly stitch (page 85)
- Perle cotton #8 thread

B. Colonial knot (page 82)
- Perle cotton #8 thread

SEAM TREATMENT D

A
B
C
D

A. Colonial knot (page 82)
- Perle cotton #8 thread

B. Stab stitch (page 91)
- Perle cotton #8 thread

C. Stab stitch (page 91)
- Perle cotton #8 thread

D. Colonial knot (page 82)
- Perle cotton #8 thread

SEAM TREATMENT E

A
B
C
D

A. Colonial knot (page 82)
- Perle cotton #8 thread

B. Stab stitch (page 91)
- Perle cotton #8 thread

C. Colonial knot (page 82)
- Perle cotton #8 thread

D. Lazy daisy stitch (page 87)
- Perle cotton #8 thread

SEAM TREATMENT F

A. Stab stitch (page 91)
- Perle cotton #8 thread

B. Colonial knot (page 82)
- Perle cotton #8 thread

SEAM TREATMENT G

A. Colonial knot (page 82)
- Perle cotton #8 thread

B. Stab stitch (page 91)
- Perle cotton #8 thread

C. Lazy daisy stitch (page 87)
- Perle cotton #8 thread

D. Feather stitch (page 84)
- Perle cotton #8 thread

E. Lazy daisy stitch (page 87)
- Perle cotton #8 thread

F. Stab stitch (page 91)
- Perle cotton #8 thread

G. Colonial knot (page 82)
- Perle cotton #8 thread

Making the Back Panel

1. Trace the perimeter lines of Pattern 3 (pullout page P3) onto the right side of the backing fabric.

2. Fuse the fleece to the wrong side of the backing fabric.

3. Trim on the cutting line.

Adding the Lining

1. Trace the perimeter lines of the front panel onto the lining fabric.

2. Trim the lining fabric on the cutting line.

3. Place the lining fabric face down on the work surface. Lay the embroidered panel right side up on the lining fabric. Align the edges and baste around the perimeter of the panel.

4. Trace the perimeter lines of the back panel onto the lining fabric. Trim on the cutting line.

5. Lay the lining fabric right side down on the work surface. Lay the backing fabric right side up on the lining fabric. Align the edges and baste around the perimeter of the back panel.

6. Mark diagonal lines 1″ apart on the back panel.

7. Machine or hand quilt along the marked lines.

Assembly

1. Cut an 11″ section of the twill tape. Fold the tape in half lengthwise. Place the folded tape over the top of the embroidered panel, enclosing the raw edges. Making sure that the tape is even on both the front and back, machine stitch the tape a scant ⅛″ from the tape's edge. Trim off the excess twill tape.

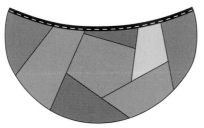

Machine stitch tape.

2. Place the back panel of the pouch with the lining fabric facing you on the work surface.

3. Lay the embroidered front panel right side up on the back panel.

> **NOTE**
> The front panel is slightly larger than the back panel.

4. Align the rounded seams of the pouch.

5. Using a scant ¼″ seam allowance, machine stitch around the rounded edge of the pouch, leaving the top open.

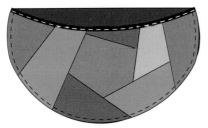

Machine stitch around rounded edge of pouch, leaving top open.

6. Cut a 21″ section of the twill tape. Fold the tape in half lengthwise and place the folded tape over the domed shape of the pouch, enclosing the raw edges; pin.

7. Make sure the tape is even on both the front and back; then machine stitch in place a scant ⅛″ from the edge of the tape to join the front and pack pouch panels. Trim off the excess twill tape.

Panels joined, leaving top open

8. Measure the circumference of your waist (yes, I know this is scary!) and add a yard to your measurement. Cut the twill tape to the final measurement.

9. Find the center of the length of the tape by folding it half widthwise. Match the center of the tape with the middle of the top edge of the back panel. Pin in place.

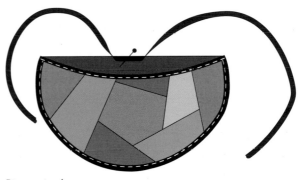

Pin tape in place.

10. Fold the twill tape in half widthwise and begin stitching the tape from 1 end, a scant ⅛″ from the edge.

11. Continue stitching until you reach the edge of the pouch. Enclose the raw edges of the top of the pouch inside the folded tape.

12. Continue stitching the tape until you reach the end.

13. Knot both ends of the tape and trim any loose threads.

14. Use contrasting threads to embroider the tape with a feather stitch.

Summer Slippers

Finished sizes: 4½″ × 10″
4½″ × 10¾″
4½″ × 11¼″

A perfect gift for a friend who has everything!

FABRIC AND SUPPLIES

- Assorted fabrics at least 4″ × 7″
- 2 pieces of foundation fabric 10″ × 10″
- 2 pieces of lining fabric 10″ × 10″ for toe
- 2 pieces of lightweight fusible fleece 10″ × 10″ for toe (I use Vilene H630 by Pellon.)
- 2 pieces of fabric 8″ × 14″ for upper sole
- 2 pieces of lightweight fusible fleece 8″ × 14″ for upper sole (I use Vilene H630 by Pellon.)
- 2 pieces of nonslip matting 8″ × 14″
- 2 pieces of batting 8″ × 14″ for lower sole

NEEDLES AND THREADS

- Milliners #03 needle for

  Perle cotton #8 thread

  Embroidery floss
- Milliners #09 needle for

  Nymo beading thread
- Chenille #22 needle for

  2mm, 4mm, and 7mm silk ribbons

EMBELLISHMENTS

- Mother of pearl buttons
- Pearl rice and round beads
- Silver beads
- 2 pieces of rickrack each 9″

Fabrics, needles, threads, and nonslip matting

Construction

Pattern includes ¼″ seam allowance.

Making the Toe Panels

Use Pattern 4 (pullout page P1) for the toe panels.

1. Follow the foundation piecing method (page 10) to complete the toe panels.

2. Follow the stitch maps (pages 26 and 27) to complete the seam treatments.

3. Trim the completed toe panels on the cutting line. Make 2.

Stitch Maps

SEAM TREATMENT A

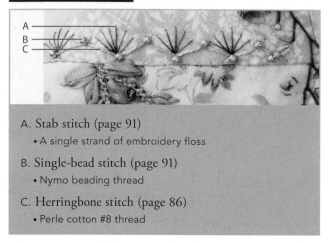

A. Stab stitch (page 91)
  • A single strand of embroidery floss

B. Single-bead stitch (page 91)
  • Nymo beading thread

C. Herringbone stitch (page 86)
  • Perle cotton #8 thread

SEAM TREATMENT B

A. Single-bead button (page 91)
  • Nymo beading thread

SEAM TREATMENT C

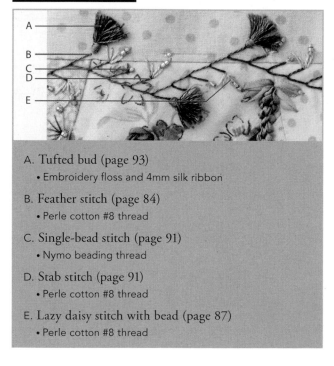

A. Tufted bud (page 93)
  • Embroidery floss and 4mm silk ribbon

B. Feather stitch (page 84)
  • Perle cotton #8 thread

C. Single-bead stitch (page 91)
  • Nymo beading thread

D. Stab stitch (page 91)
  • Perle cotton #8 thread

E. Lazy daisy stitch with bead (page 87)
  • Perle cotton #8 thread

SEAM TREATMENT D

A. Lazy daisy stitch (page 87)
  • 4mm silk ribbon

B. Palestrina knot stitch (page 88)
  • Perle cotton #8 thread

C. Chain stitch rose (page 82)
  • 4mm silk ribbon

D. Colonial knot (page 82)
  • 4mm silk ribbon

SEAM TREATMENT E

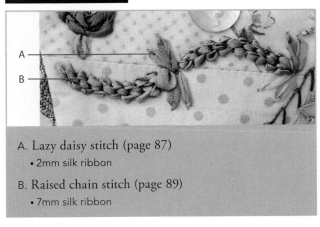

A. Lazy daisy stitch (page 87)
  • 2mm silk ribbon

B. Raised chain stitch (page 89)
  • 7mm silk ribbon

PIECE 3

A. Single-bead stitch (page 91)
  • Nymo beading thread

B. Stab stitch (page 91)
  • Perle cotton #8 thread

Making the Slipper Soles

Use Pattern 5 (pullout page P1) for the slipper soles.

1. Trace the cutting lines and markings of the slipper soles onto the upper sole fabric. Fuse the fleece to the wrong side of the upper sole fabric. Trim to the cutting line.

2. Mark diagonal lines 2″ apart on the right side of the upper sole; machine quilt.

3. Trace the cutting lines onto the nonslip matting. Trim to the cutting lines.

4. Baste the batting to the wrong side of the nonslip matting for each sole.

Adding the Lining

1. Trace and trim the 2 toe panel linings on the cutting line.

2. On the wrong side of each lining, mark a line at each corner ¼″ from the edges. Make a pencil mark (*) at the intersection as shown.

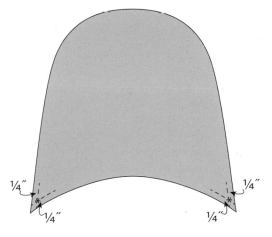

¼″   ¼″

¼″   ¼″

Mark * at each corner.

3. Machine stitch the rickrack in place on the right side of the fabric along the lower edge of the toe panels.

4. Lay the upper toe panel right side up on the work surface. Place the toe lining right side down on the upper toe panel.

5. Align the edges and stitch along the lower edge of the toe panel from * to *. Clip the curve.

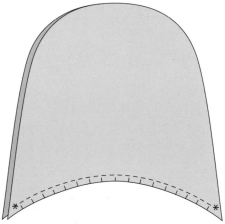

Stitch along lower edge of toe panel.

6. Turn toe panels right side out. Use a spatula to gently push out the stitch seams; press lightly.

7. You might find it helpful to baste the raw edges together using a scant ¼″ seam allowance.

8. Repeat Steps 4–7 for the other toe panel.

Assembly

1. Place the upper sole fabric right side up on the work surface. Mark the 2 *'s on the fabric.

2. Place the toe panel right side down on the upper sole.

3. Align the edges and stitch from * to *.

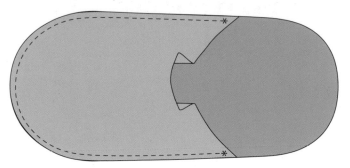

Stitch from * to *.

4. Place the batting and nonslip matting section on the work surface with the nonslip matting facing you.

5. Place the upper section of the slipper right side down on the nonslip matting.

6. Pin and stitch around the slipper sole, leaving a small opening on the side for turning.

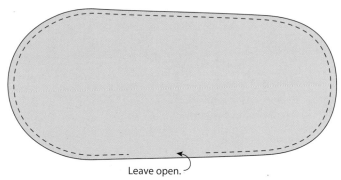

Leave open.

Stitch around slipper sole, leaving small opening for turning.

7. Gently turn the slipper through. Use a spatula to push out the seams.

8. Slipstitch the opening closed.

9. Gently press the slipper's outer edge.

Upcycled Wool Bag

Finished size: 13″ × 13″

This bag is a creative way
to upcycle wool scraps.

FABRIC AND SUPPLIES

- Assorted wool scraps at least 6″ × 6″

- 2 pieces of lining fabric 9½″ × 14½″

- 1 piece of nonwoven fusible fabric stabilizer 15″ × 30″

- 1 piece of nonwoven fusible fabric stabilizer 6″ × 32″

- Lightweight cardboard (such as poster board) for English paper piecing

- Small wooden handles

- Template plastic

- Fine-point pencil

Fabrics, threads, and bag handles

Construction

Making the Bag

Use Pattern 6 (pullout page P1) for the apple core shapes.

1. Trace the apple core shape onto template plastic.

2. Trace around the template onto the cardboard with a fine-point pencil. Cut on this line.

3. Use the template to cut out 35 core shapes from the wool fabric, adding a ½″ seam allowance on all sides.

4. Center and pin a cardboard piece on the wrong side of a wool fabric piece.

5. Use a sewing thread and a milliners needle to baste the raw edges of the wool fabric to the back of the paper piece.

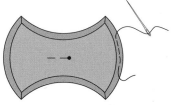

Baste raw edges of wool fabric down.

6. Thread a needle with a single thickness of matching thread and make a knot on 1 end.

7. Select 2 fabric-covered pieces and make a small crease at the center point of each of the 2 edges you'll be sewing together.

8. Hold the 2 pieces together with right sides facing. Starting at a corner, sew the pieces together with an overcast or whip stitch. Rotate the top piece as you sew, matching the center points and corners, as shown.

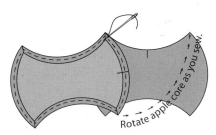

Sew fabric-covered pieces together.

Use Pattern 7 (pullout page P1) for the layout plan.

> **NOTE**
> There are a total of 35 apple core shapes—27 are used in the bag layout and 8 are used in the lining.

9. Do not remove the basting stitches and cardboard until the bag panel is complete.

10. With a warm iron, press the bag panel well from the front.

11. Place the bag panel face down on the ironing board and carefully remove the basting stitches and cardboard from the bag panel.

12. Trim the stabilizer to the same size as the bag panel. Following the manufacturer's instructions, fuse the 15″ × 30″ piece of fabric stabilizer to the wrong side of the bag panel.

13. Follow the stitch maps (pages 32–39) to complete the bag panel.

Stitch Maps

A. Lazy daisy stitch (page 87)
  • 4mm silk ribbon

B. Stem stitch (page 92)
  • Silk perle #8 thread

C. Ribbon stitch (page 89)
  • 4mm silk ribbon

A. Palestrina knot stitch (page 88)
  • 2mm silk ribbon

B. Lazy daisy stitch (page 87)
  • 4mm silk ribbon

C. Fishbone stitch (page 84)
  • 4mm silk ribbon

A. Colonial knot (page 82)
  • 4mm silk ribbon

B. Lazy daisy stitch (page 87)
  • 4mm silk ribbon

C. Stab stitch (page 91)
  • Silk perle #8 thread

D. Feather stitch (page 84)
  • Chenille thread

SEAM TREATMENT D

A. Ribbon stitch (page 89)
- 4mm silk ribbon

B. Feather stitch (page 84)
- 4mm silk ribbon

C. Stab stitch (page 91)
- 4mm silk ribbon

SEAM TREATMENT E

A. Bullion lazy daisy stitch (page 81)
- 4mm silk ribbon

B. Twisted chain stitch (page 93)
- 2mm silk ribbon

SEAM TREATMENT F

A. Stab stitch (page 91)
- Perle cotton #12 thread

B. Lazy daisy stitch (page 87)
- Perle cotton #8 thread

C. Lazy daisy stitch flower (page 87)
- 4mm silk ribbon

D. Stem stitch (page 92)
- Perle cotton #8 thread

SEAM TREATMENT G

A. Lazy daisy stitch (page 87)
- Perle cotton #8 thread

B. Ruched rose (page 90)
- 4mm silk ribbon

C. Herringbone stitch (page 86)
- Perle cotton #8 thread

D. Stab stitch (page 91)
- Perle cotton #8 thread

E. Lazy daisy stitch (page 87)
- 4mm silk ribbon

SEAM TREATMENT H

A. Stab stitch (page 91)
  • Perle cotton #12 thread

B. Lazy daisy stitch (page 87)
  • 4mm silk ribbon

C. Stem stitch (page 92)
  • 2mm silk ribbon

D. Fly stitch leaf (page 85)
  • 4mm silk ribbon

SEAM TREATMENT I

A. Lazy daisy stitch (page 87)
  • 2mm silk ribbon

B. Chevron stitch (page 82)
  • Perle cotton #8 thread

C. Lazy daisy stitch (page 87)
  • 4mm silk ribbon

SEAM TREATMENT J

A. Stab stitch (page 91)
  • Silk perle #12 thread·

B. Spiderweb rose (page 91)
  • 7mm silk ribbon

C. Ruched rose (page 90)
  • 7mm silk ribbon

D. Ribbon stitch (page 89)
  • 7mm silk ribbon

E. Ribbon stitch (page 89)
  • 4mm silk ribbon

F. Lazy daisy stitch (page 87)
  • 7mm silk ribbon

SEAM TREATMENT K

A
B
C
D
E

A. Loop stitch and flower (page 87)
  • 4mm silk ribbon

B. Ribbon stitch (page 89)
  • 4mm silk ribbon

C. Lazy daisy stitch (page 87)
  • 4mm silk ribbon

D. Stab stitch couching (page 92)
  • 4mm silk ribbon

E. Ruched rose (page 90)
  • 4mm silk ribbon

SEAM TREATMENT L

A
B
C
D

A. Ribbon stitch (page 89)
  • 4mm silk ribbon

B. Padded stab stitch (page 88)
  • 7mm silk ribbon

C. Palestrina knot stitch (page 88)
  • Perle cotton #8 thread

D. Bullion lazy daisy stitch (page 81)
  • Perle cotton #8 thread

SEAM TREATMENT M

A
B
C

A. Lazy daisy stitch (page 87)
  • 4mm silk ribbon

B. Colonial knot (page 82)
  • 4mm silk ribbon

C. Stem stitch (page 92)
  • Perle cotton #8 thread

SEAM TREATMENT N

A. Colonial knot (page 82)
- 4mm silk ribbon

B. Stem stitch (page 92)
- Perle cotton #8 thread

C. Looped ribbon stitch (page 87)
- 4mm silk ribbon

SEAM TREATMENT O

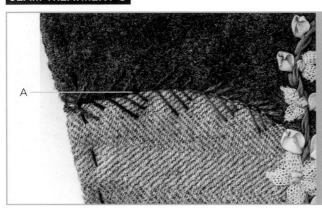

A. Fly stitch (page 85)
- Perle cotton #8 thread

SEAM TREATMENT P

A. Fly stitch leaf (page 85)
- 4mm silk ribbon

SEAM TREATMENT Q

A. Lazy daisy stitch (page 87)
- Tulle ribbon

B. Stem stitch (page 92)
- 2mm silk ribbon

C. Lazy daisy stitch (page 87)
- 4mm silk ribbon

D. Ribbon stitch (page 89)
- 7mm silk ribbon

E. Colonial knot (page 82)
- 4mm silk ribbon

SEAM TREATMENT R

A —
B —

A. Feather stitch (page 84)
  • 4mm silk ribbon

B. Free-form flower with beaded
   center (page 86)
  • 7mm silk ribbon

SEAM TREATMENT S

A —

A. Feather stitch (page 84)
  • 4mm silk ribbon

SEAM TREATMENT T

A —
B —
C —
D —

E —

A. Stab stitch (page 91)
  • Perle cotton #8 thread

B. Colonial knot (page 82)
  • Perle cotton #8 thread

C. Feather stitch (page 84)
  • Perle cotton #12 thread

D. Whipped chain stitch
   (page 94)
  • Perle cotton #8 thread

E. Colonial knot (page 82)
  • Perle cotton #12 thread

SEAM TREATMENT U

A —

A. Lazy daisy stitch flower
   (page 87)
  • 4mm silk ribbon

SEAM TREATMENT V

A —

A. Stab stitch (page 91)
• Perle cotton #8 thread

SEAM TREATMENT W

A —
B —
C —

A. Stem stitch (page 92)
• Perle cotton #8 thread

B. Padded stab stitch (page 88)
• 4mm silk ribbon

C. Colonial knot (page 82)
• 7mm silk ribbon

SEAM TREATMENT X

A —

A. Delphinium (page 83)
• See stitch dictionary for threads.

SEAM TREATMENT Y

A —

A. Fly stitch leaf (page 85)
• 4mm silk ribbon

SEAM TREATMENT Z

A. Ribbon stitch flower (page 89)
- 4mm silk ribbon

B. Stab stitch (page 91)
- Chenille thread

SEAM TREATMENT ZZ

A. Lazy daisy stitch (page 87)
- 4mm silk ribbon

B. Loop stitch and flower (page 88)
- 7mm silk ribbon

C. Whipped chain stitch (page 94)
- Perle cotton #8 thread and 4mm silk ribbon

D. Feather stitch (page 84)
- Perle cotton #12 thread

E. Colonial knot (page 82)
- Perle cotton #8 thread

F. Ribbon stitch flower (page 89)
- 7mm silk ribbon

CLOSING SEAM TREATMENT BASE

A. Feather stitch (page 84)
- 4mm silk ribbon

Preparing the Lining

1. Join the remaining 8 apple core shapes.

2. Trim the stabilizer to the same size as the apple core shape. Press well and then remove the basting stitches and cardboard. Fuse the 6″ × 32″ piece of fabric stabilizer to the wrong side of the apple core shapes.

3. Stitch the first and last apple cores together to form a circle. Use the top row of the layout plan to identify the placement of the center front and center back. Mark with pins.

4. Place the 2 lining pieces right sides together. Stitch along the sides and lower edge, leaving a generous opening for turning. Fold in half to locate the center front and center back. Mark with a pencil or make a crease at the top of the lining fabric.

Stitch along sides and lower edge of lining fabric.

5. Turn the lining right side out. Place the lining into the circle of apple cores. Pin together at the center front and center back.

6. Align the circle of apple cores just over the top edge of the lining, making sure that the raw edges of the lining fabrics are not visible.

7. Machine stitch along the lower edge of the apple cores, joining the lining fabric to the circle of apple cores.

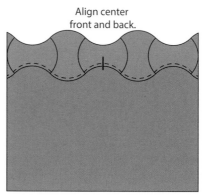

Join circle of apple cores to top of lining.

Assembly

Use Pattern 7 (pullout page P1) for the layout.

1. Join the side panels and the base of the bag by connecting corresponding numbered edges on Pattern 7.

2. Drop the outer bag into the lining, right sides together.

3. Align the apple core shapes along the bag's top edge.

4. Whipstitch the lining and outer bags together.

5. Turn the bag right side out through the opening left in the lining.

6. Gently push out the edges with a spatula.

7. Slipstitch the lining opening closed.

8. Press along the turned edge.

9. Topstitch with a perle cotton #8 thread around the top of the bag.

10. Attach the handles in place as desired.

Hexagon Purse

Finished size: 7″ × 8″ (without handles)

A "crazy" hexagon purse is a perfect addition to the collection of all the hexagon enthusiasts out there.

FABRIC AND SUPPLIES

- Assorted fabric scraps at least 5″ × 8″

- 2 pieces of foundation fabric 12″ × 12″

- 2 pieces of lightweight fusible fleece 12″ × 12″ (I use Vilene H630 by Pellon.)

- 2 pieces of backing fabric 9″ × 9″

- 2 pieces of fabric 3⅛″ × 17⅝″ for gusset

- 2 template plastic 4″ hexagons

- 2 pieces of template plastic 2½″ × 2½″ for gusset

- 3 pieces of template plastic 2½″ × 4″ for gusset

- 2 pieces of fabric 2½″ × 14½″ for handles

- 2 pieces of poly boning (Birch 012927) 1″ × 14″ for handles

- 4 fabric circles 3″ in diameter for yo-yos

- 1 small Clover yo-yo maker (optional)

- Glue stick

- 2 bulldog clamps

NEEDLES AND THREADS

- Milliners #03 needle for

  Perle cotton #8 and #12 thread

  Embroidery floss

- Milliners #09 needle for

  Nymo beading thread

- Chenille #22 needle for

  2mm, 4mm, and 7mm silk ribbons

  Silk perle #8 thread

  Twisted rayon thread 4mm

  Velvet thread

  Gold metallic thread

EMBELLISHMENTS

- Small sequins

- Seed beads

- Selection of assorted beads

- 2″ heart-shaped lace motif

- 3 leaf-shaped mother-of-pearl buttons

- Small heart-shaped button and round bead for spider

- Small piece of lace

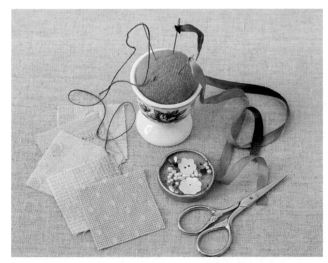

Fabrics, buttons, and beads

Construction

Making the Front and Back Panels

Use Pattern 8 (pullout page P3) for the panels.

1. Follow the foundation piecing method (page 10) to complete the front and back panels.

2. Follow the stitch maps (pages 44–46) to complete the seam treatments. Use Treatments *A–E* and Piece 2 for the front panel and Treatments *F–J* for the back panel.

3. Trim the completed front and back panels to the cutting line (4″ hexagon).

Stitch Maps

SEAM TREATMENT A

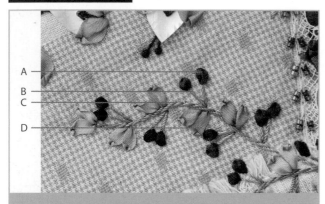

A. Padded stab stitch (page 88)
- 4mm silk ribbon

B. Stab stitch (page 91)
- Silk perle #8 thread

C. Stem stitch (page 92)
- Perle cotton #8 thread

D. Ribbon stitch (page 89)
- 4mm silk ribbon

SEAM TREATMENT B

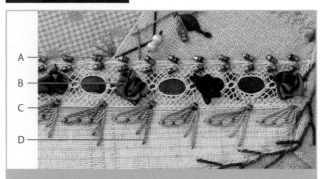

A. Fly stitch with beads (page 85)
- Perle cotton #12 thread

B. Ruched rose (page 90)
- 7mm silk ribbon

C. Buttonhole wing stitch (page 81)
- Silk perle #8 thread

D. Stab stitch (page 91)
- Silk perle #8 thread

SEAM TREATMENT C

A. Stab stitch (page 91)
- Silk perle #8 thread

B. Chevron stitch with beads (page 82)
- Perle cotton #8 thread

C. Herringbone stitch (page 86)
- Perle cotton #8 thread

D. Lazy daisy stitch with bead (page 87)
- Silk perle #8 thread

E. Bullion lazy daisy stitch (page 81)
- 2mm silk ribbon

SEAM TREATMENT D

A. Colonial knot stitch (page 82)
- Perle cotton #8 thread

B. Stab stitch (page 91)
- Perle cotton #8 thread

C. Button (page 81)
- Perle cotton #8 thread

D. Ribbon stitch (page 89)
- 7mm silk ribbon

SEAM TREATMENT E

A. Five-petal flower (page 85)
- 7mm silk ribbon

B. Stab stitch (page 91)
- Velvet thread

C. Single-bead stitch (page 91)
- Nymo beading thread

D. Lazy daisy stitch (page 87)
- Twisted rayon thread

PIECE 2

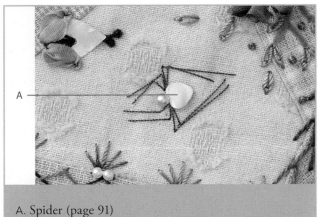

A. Spider (page 91)

See stitch dictionary for threads.

SEAM TREATMENT F

A. Fern stitch (page 84)
- Perle cotton #8 thread

B. Feather stitch (page 84)
- Silk perle #8 thread

C. Beaded leaf (page 80)
- Nymo beading thread

D. Single bead stitch (page 91)
- Nymo beading thread

SEAM TREATMENT G

A. Loop stitch and flower (page 88)
- 7mm silk ribbon

B. Colonial knot (page 82)
- Twisted rayon thread

C. Ribbon stitch (page 89)
- 4mm silk ribbon

D. Lazy daisy stitch (page 87)
- 4mm silk ribbon

E. Stab stitch (page 91)
- Silk perle #8 thread

F. Knotted fly stitch (page 86)
- 4mm twisted rayon thread

SEAM TREATMENT H

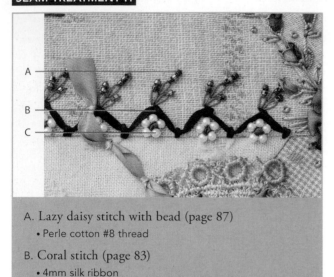

A. Lazy daisy stitch with bead (page 87)
- Perle cotton #8 thread

B. Coral stitch (page 83)
- 4mm silk ribbon

C. Beaded forget-me-not (page 80)
- Nymo beading thread

SEAM TREATMENT I

A. Stab stitch couching (page 92)
- 7mm silk ribbon

B. Ruched rose (page 90)
- 7mm silk ribbon

C. Single bead stitch (page 91)
- Nymo beading thread

D. Ribbon stitch (page 89)
- 4mm silk ribbon

SEAM TREATMENT J

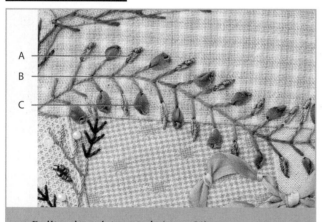

A. Bullion lazy daisy stitch (page 81)
- Silk perle #8 thread

B. Fly stitch (page 85)
- Perle cotton #8 thread

C. Ribbon stitch (page 89)
- 4mm silk ribbon

Adding the Backing

1. Apply the glue along the edges and center of a template plastic hexagon.

2. Lay the front panel hexagon, embellished side up, on the glued surface of the template plastic hexagon. Align all sides and apply light pressure so the glue makes contact with the lightweight fusible fleece.

Use Pattern 9 (pullout page P3) to cut out the backing fabric.

> **NOTE**
> The backing fabric hexagon should be 1˝ larger than the embellished hexagon all the way around.

3. Lay the backing hexagon, right side down, on the work surface.

4. Center the embellished front panel hexagon, right side up, on the backing fabric.

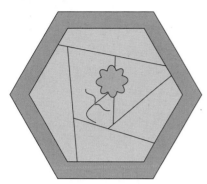

Center finished front panel hexagon on backing fabric.

5. Working on one side of the hexagon at a time, trim the exposed backing fabric back to ¾″.

6. Fold the backing fabric in half, so the raw edge aligns with the raw edge of the embellished hexagon. Finger-press.

7. Fold the backing fabric again, so it now lies folded over the embellished hexagon with the raw edges enclosed.

8. Use small bulldog clips to hold the fabric in place.

Use small bulldog clips to hold fabric in place.

9. Stitch down the folded edge of the backing fabric using a blind hem or appliqué stitch. Continue working on one side at a time.

10. Feather stitch around the hexagon with a perle cotton #8 thread of your choice.

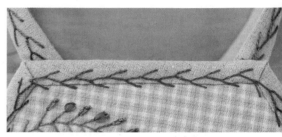

Feather stitch along folded edge.

11. Repeat Steps 2–10 for the second hexagon panel.

Preparing the Gusset

1. Trim the sharp edges of the gusset template plastic pieces.

2. Place the 2 gusset pieces right sides together.

3. Using a ¼″ seam allowance, stitch around 3 sides of the gusset, leaving a short side open.

4. Clip the corners and turn the gusset to the right side.

5. Gently push out the corners with a knitting needle.

6. Gently push out the seams with a spatula and press lightly.

7. Insert a 2½″ × 2½″ piece of template plastic firmly in the gusset panel.

8. Machine stitch as close to the inserted template plastic as possible.

9. Complete the gusset panel by following the sequence shown below. Working from left to right, insert each template plastic piece and then machine stitch each section.

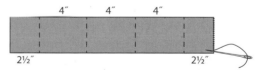

Sequence for completing gusset

10. Fold the remaining raw edges inward and slipstitch closed.

Preparing the Handles

1. Fold a piece of the 2½″ × 14½″ fabric in half lengthwise, right sides together.

2. Stitch the long sides using a scant ¼″ seam.

3. Turn right side out.

4. Press well, making sure the seam is centered on the wrong side of the handle.

5. Insert the length of poly boning.

6. Featherstitch along the right side of the handle.

7. Repeat Steps 1–6 for the second handle.

Making the Yo-Yos

1. Make 4 yo-yos using the instructions below or following the instructions on the yo-yo maker.

2. For each fabric circle, turn under the edge ¼″. Press.

Turn under edge.

3. Hand baste ⅛″ from the folded edge.

4. Pull the thread to gather the circle; tie the thread.

Pull thread and tie off.

Assembly

1. With the right side of the handles facing outward, position the raw edge of the handle 1″ below the top edge of the inside of the hexagon panel.

2. Slipstitch in place.

3. Cover the raw edges of the purse handle with a yo-yo and slipstitch in place.

Attach handles to inside of hexagon panels.

4. With the wrong sides of the panel and gusset facing each other, join them with a glove stitch (page 86) using perle cotton #12 thread.

5. Follow the diagram for joining the pieces.

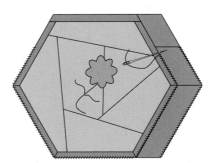

Join gusset to purse front and back.

6. Repeat Steps 1–5 to join the second hexagon panel.

Wool Tea Cozy

Finished size: 8½″ × 11″

Both functional and beautiful, a crazy wool tea cozy will add glamour to any occasion.

Wool, ribbon, and lining fabric

Construction

Pattern includes ¼″ seam allowance.

Making the Front and Back Panels

Use Pattern 10 (pullout page P2) for the front and back panels.

1. Follow the foundation piecing method (page 10) Steps 1–7 for the front and back panels.

2. Begin laying out wool pieces to form the crazy quilt design.

3. Simply lay each piece of wool on the foundation fabric, allowing a ½″ overlap onto the adjoining piece. *Note: Raw edges will be covered by seam treatments.*

3. Baste in place along the seamlines.

4. Follow the stitch maps (pages 51–53) to complete the seam treatments. Use Treatments *A–G* for the front panel and Treatments *H–N* for the back panel.

5. Remove the basting stitches.

6. Trim the completed front and back panels to the cutting line.

Stitch Maps

SEAM TREATMENT A

A. Plume stitch (page 88)
- 7mm silk ribbon

B. Stab stitch (page 91)
- 4mm silk ribbon

C. Wheatear stitch (page 93)
- Twisted rayon thread

D. Feather stitch (page 84)
- Perle cotton #12 thread

E. Colonial knot (page 82)
- Perle cotton #8 thread

SEAM TREATMENT B

A. Chain stitch (page 82)
- 2mm silk ribbon

B. Bullion lazy daisy stitch (page 81)
- Perle cotton #8 thread

C. Stab stitch (page 91)
- Silk perle #12 thread

D. Colonial knot (page 82)
- Silk perle #12 thread

E. Lazy daisy stitch (page 87)
- Perle cotton #12 thread

F. Feather stitch (page 84)
- Silk perle #8 thread

SEAM TREATMENT C

A. Stab stitch leaf (page 92)
- Velvet thread

B. Fly stitch (page 85)
- Perle cotton #8 thread

SEAM TREATMENT D

A. Delphinium (page 83)
- See stitch dictionary for threads.

SEAM TREATMENT E

A. Herringbone stitch (page 86)
- Perle cotton #8 thread

B. Ribbon stitch (page 89)
- 4mm silk ribbon

C. Colonial knot (page 82)
- 4mm silk ribbon

SEAM TREATMENT F

A. Lazy daisy stitch (page 87)
  • Perle cotton #12 thread

B. Stab stitch (page 91)
  • Perle cotton #12 thread

C. Feather stitch (page 84)
  • 4mm silk ribbon

SEAM TREATMENT G

A. Stab stitch (page 91)
  • A single strand
    of embroidery thread

B. Lazy daisy stitch (page 87)
  • Silk perle #8 thread

C. Colonial knot (page 82)
  • Perle cotton #8 thread

D. Stem stitch (page 92)
  • Perle cotton #8 thread

E. Lazy daisy stitch (page 87)
  • 2mm silk ribbon

F. Ruched silk ribbon garland
   (page 90)
  • 13mm silk ribbon

SEAM TREATMENT H

A. Colonial knot (page 82)
  • Perle cotton #8 thread

B. Feather stitch (page 84)
  • Perle cotton #8 thread

C. Lazy daisy stitch (page 87)
  • 4mm silk ribbon

D. Lazy daisy stitch (page 87)
  • Tulle ribbon

E. Ribbon stitch (page 89)
  • 4mm silk ribbon

F. Lazy daisy stitch flower
   (page 87)
  • 7mm silk ribbon

G. Lazy daisy stitch flower
   (page 87)
  • Tulle ribbon

SEAM TREATMENT I

A. Lazy daisy stitch (page 87)
  • Perle cotton #8 thread

B. Ruched silk ribbon
   garland (page 90)
  • 7 mm silk ribbon

C. Colonial knot (page 82)
  • Perle cotton #8 thread

D. Stab stitch couching
   (page 92)
  • Perle cotton #8 thread

PIECE 3

A. Colonial knot (page 82)
  • Perle cotton #8 thread

B. Lazy daisy stitch (page 87)
  • 4mm silk ribbon

SEAM TREATMENT J

A
B
C

A. Stab stitch (page 91)
  • Silk perle #8 thread

B. Ribbon stitch (page 89)
  • 4mm silk ribbon

C. Wheatear stitch (page 93)
  • Silk perle #8 thread

SEAM TREATMENT K

A
B

A. Cretan stitch (page 83)
  • 4mm silk ribbon

B. Ruched rose (page 90)
  • 4mm silk ribbon

SEAM TREATMENT L

A
B
C

A. Stab stitch couching (page 92)
  • Silk perle #8 thread

B. Fly stitch leaf (page 85)
  • 4mm silk ribbon

C. Colonial knot (page 82)
  • 7mm silk ribbon

SEAM TREATMENT M

A
B
C
D
E
F

A. Fly stitch leaf (page 85)
  • 4mm silk ribbon

B. Colonial knot (page 82)
  • Perle cotton #8 thread

C. Fly stitch (page 85)
  • Silk perle #8 thread

D. Bullion knot (page 81)
  • Silk perle #8 thread

E. Ruched rose (page 90)
  • 4mm silk ribbon

F. Feather stitch (page 84)
  • 4mm silk ribbon

SEAM TREATMENT N

A
B
C
D

A. Stab stitch (page 91)
  • Tulle ribbon

B. Lazy daisy stitch (page 87)
  • 7mm silk ribbon

C. Ribbon stitch (page 89)
  • 4mm silk ribbon

D. Stem stitch (page 92)
  • 2mm silk ribbon

Assembly

1. Trace the perimeter lines of the tea cozy onto the 2 pieces of lining fabric. Trim on the cutting line.

2. Lay the lining pieces on top of each other with the right sides facing each other.

3. Pin and sew the lining panels around the domed shape only. Leave a 5″ opening at the top for turning.

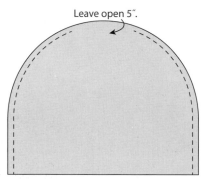

Sew around domed part of lining panels.

4. Place a tea cozy panel right side up on the work surface. Place the pompom trim's insertion tape flush with the raw edge of the panel and with the pompoms facing the center. Stitch the length of trim in place, staying as close as possible to the pompoms.

5. Lay the outer panels on top of each other with the right sides facing.

6. Pin and sew the outer panels together around the domed shape.

7. Turn the outer panels right side out. Use a spatula to gently push out the seam. Lightly press the turned outer seam.

8. Push the outer tea cozy panels inside the lining fabrics with right sides facing.

9. Pin together the bottom edges of the outer panels and lining fabrics. Stitch to close.

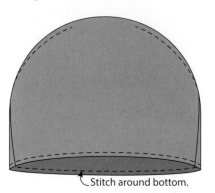

Sew lining and tea cozy panels together at bottom edge.

10. Turn the tea cozy right side out by gently pushing the embroidered panels through the turning gap.

11. Use a spatula to gently push out the seams.

12. Slipstitch the turning opening closed.

13. Push the lining fabric into the domed shape and press edge.

Glasses Purse

Finished size: 7″ × 4″

This glasses purse could easily double as a travel sewing caddy.

FABRIC AND SUPPLIES

- Assorted fabric scraps at least 4″ × 5″
- 2 pieces of foundation fabric 6″ × 9″
- 2 pieces of lining fabric 6″ × 9″
- 2 pieces of lightweight fusible fleece 6″ × 9″ (I use Vilene H630 by Pellon.)
- 1 piece of backing fabric 6″ × 9″
- 1 rectangular purse frame 2½″ × 7″
- 1 piece of embroidered doily at least 4″ × 5″

NEEDLES AND THREADS

- Milliners #03 needle for

    Perle cotton #8 thread

    Perle cotton #12 thread

- Milliners #09 needle for

    Nymo beading thread

- Chenille #22 needle for

    Gold metallic thread

EMBELLISHMENTS

- Seed beads
- Small pearl beads
- 2 small heart-shaped buttons
- 1 round button

Fabrics, doily, buttons, and beads

Construction

Pattern includes ¼″ seam allowance.

Making the Front Panel

Use Pattern 11 (pullout page P3) for the front panel.

1. Follow the foundation piecing method (page 10) to complete the front panel.

2. Follow the stitch maps (page 57) to complete the seam treatments.

3. Trim the completed front panel on the cutting line.

Stitch Maps

PIECES 1 AND 4

A.
B.

A. Lazy daisy stitch (page 87)
  • Gold metallic thread

B. Single-bead stitch (page 91)
  • Nymo beading thread

SEAM TREATMENT A

A
B
C
D

A. Stab stitch (page 91)
  • Silk perle #8 thread

B. Feather stitch with beads (page 84)
  • Perle cotton #8 thread

C. Lazy daisy stitch (page 87)
  • Perle cotton #12 thread

D. Single-bead stitch (page 91)
  • Nymo beading thread

SEAM TREATMENT B

A

A. Single-bead button (page 91)
  • Nymo beading thread

SEAM TREATMENT C

A
B

A. Lazy daisy stitch with bead (page 87)
  • Perle cotton #12 thread

B. Stab stitch (page 91)
  • Perle cotton #12 thread

SEAM TREATMENT D

A
B
C
D

A. Beaded leaf (page 80)
  • Nymo beading thread

B. Lazy daisy stitch (page 87)
  • Perle cotton #8 thread

C. Stab stitch (page 91)
  • Perle cotton #8 thread

D. Single-bead stitch (page 91)
  • Nymo beading thread

Making the Back Panel

1. Trace the perimeter lines of the front panel onto the right side of the backing fabric.

2. Fuse the fleece to the wrong side of the back panel.

3. Trim the completed back panel to the cutting line.

Assembly

1. Trace the perimeter lines of the front panel onto the wrong sides of 1 piece of lining fabric. Mark the 2 *'s on the fabric.

2. Place the front panel and a lining piece rights sides together. Sew the top edge from * to *.

Sew top edge.

3. Repeat Steps 1 and 2 for the back panel and the other piece of lining fabric.

4. Place the front and back panels right sides together, matching the side seams.

5. Sew around the side seams of the front and back panels only from * to *.

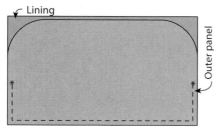

Sew around side seams.

6. Place the lining pieces right sides together, matching the side seams.

7. Sew around the extended side seams of the *lining fabric only* from * to *, leaving a 4″ opening in the lining fabrics for turning.

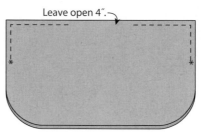

Sew around extended side seams of lining fabric.

8. Gently turn the purse right side out through the opening. Slipstitch the opening closed.

9. Open the purse frame and push the fabric into the frame.

10. With 2 strands of perle cotton #8 thread and a chenille #22 needle, use a running stitch to stitch the purse to the frame. Start at the center and work outward, going in and out of the holes in the frame.

11. Slipstitch a trim around the lower edge of the glasses purse.

Spring Flower Bag

Finished size: 8″ × 14″

This flower bag is not crazy quilting in its traditional form; however, all my favorite crazy stitches are showcased in this cathedral window technique.

Fabrics, needles, and frame accessories

Construction

Making the Embroidered Hexagons

Use Pattern 12 (pullout page P4) for the hexagons.

1. Trace the hexagon shape onto template plastic. Cut around the shape to create a hexagon template.

2. Center the hexagon template on the 6″ × 6″ center fabric. Trace around the template with a fine-tipped pencil.

3. Fuse the fleece to the wrong side of each 6″ square.

Use Pattern 13 (pullout page P4) for the petals.

4. Trace the petal shape onto template plastic. Cut around the shape to create a petal template.

5. Mark the petal shape on the hexagon drawn on the flower center fabric to clearly identify your working area. Be sure to use an erasable pencil or marking pen.

Use Pattern 15 (pullout page P4) for the layout plan.

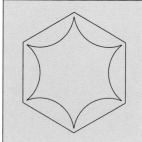

Working area inside hexagon

6. Follow the layout plan and stitch maps (pages 61–63) to complete the embroidery, staying away from the petal shapes marked on the hexagon.

7. Trim each hexagon to the cutting line.

 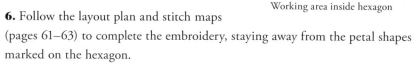

Stitch Maps

HEXAGON 1

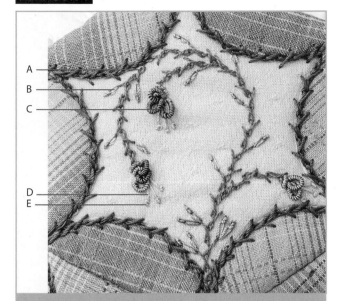

A. Twisted chain stitch (page 93)
- Silk perle #8 thread

B. Bullion lazy daisy stitch (page 81)
- Silk perle #8 thread

C. Looped bullion knot stitch (page 87)
- Silk perle #8 thread

D. Stab stitch (page 91)
- Silk perle #8 thread

E. Colonial knot (page 82)
- Silk perle #8 thread

HEXAGON 2

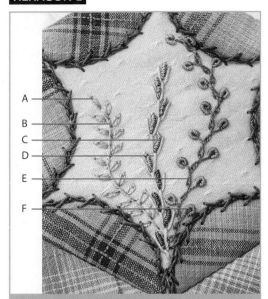

A. Lazy daisy stitch (page 87)
- Perle cotton #8 thread

B. Stem stitch (page 92)
- Perle cotton #8 thread

C. Bullion knot (page 81)
- Perle cotton #8 thread

D. Feather stitch (page 84)
- Perle cotton #8 thread

E. Twisted chain stitch (page 93)
- Perle cotton #8 thread

F. Looped bullion knot stitch (page 87)
- Perle cotton #8 thread

HEXAGON 3

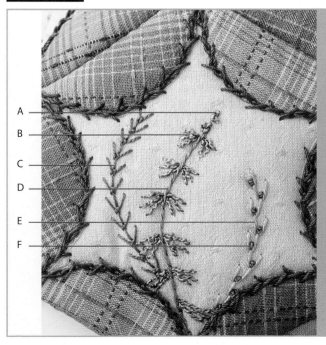

A. Colonial knot (page 82)
- Bouclé rayon thread

B. Stab stitch (page 91)
- Bouclé rayon thread

C. Knotted fly stitch (page 86)
- Perle cotton #8 thread

D. Stem stitch (page 92)
- Perle cotton #8 thread

E. Feather stitch (page 84)
- Perle cotton #8 thread

F. Colonial knot (page 82)
- Perle cotton #8 thread

HEXAGON 4

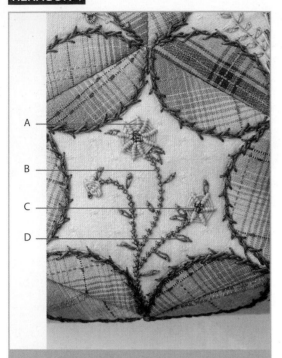

A. Woven spiderweb (page 94)
- Cotton crochet yarn

B. Palestrina stitch (page 88)
- Perle cotton #8 thread

C. Colonial knot (page 82)
- Perle cotton #8 thread

D. Bullion lazy daisy stitch (page 81)
- Perle cotton #8 thread

HEXAGON 5

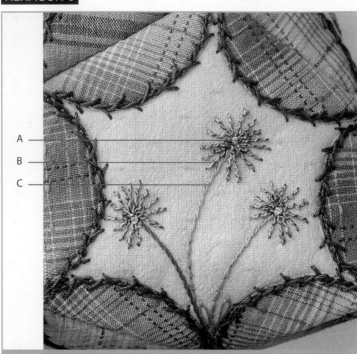

A. Colonial knot (page 82)
- Perle cotton #8 thread

B. Stab stitch (page 91)
- Bouclé rayon thread

C. Stem stitch (page 92)
- Perle cotton #8 thread

HEXAGON 6

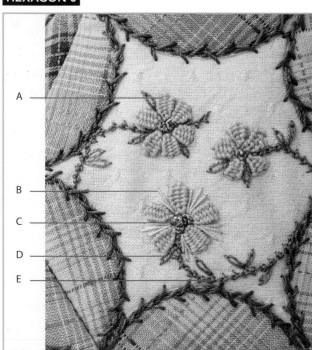

A. Woven trellis stitch (page 94)
- Cotton crochet yarn

B. Stab stitch (page 91)
- Perle cotton #8 thread

C. Colonial knot (page 82)
- Perle cotton #8 thread

D. Lazy daisy stitch (page 87)
- Perle cotton #3 thread

E. Palestrina stitch (page 88)
- Perle cotton #8 thread

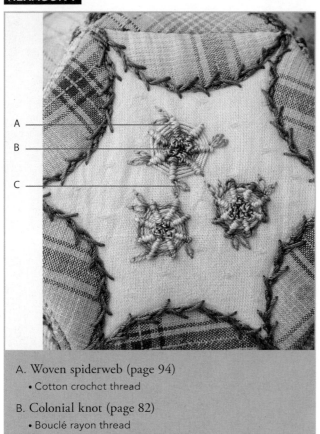

HEXAGON 7

A. Woven spiderweb (page 94)
• Cotton crochet thread

B. Colonial knot (page 82)
• Bouclé rayon thread

C. Lazy daisy stitch (page 87)
• Perle cotton #8 thread

Making the Flower Petals

Use Pattern 14 (pullout page P4) for the flower petal shape.

1. Trace the hexagon flower petal shape onto template plastic. Cut around the flower shape to create a template.

2. Use your template to trace the flower shapes onto the interfacing.

3. Pin the petal fabric to the interfacing, right sides together.

4. Machine stitch along the marked petal shape, keeping the curves smooth and round.

5. Trim fabric a ¼″ from the machine stitching.

Trim with scissors.

6. Snip into the petal intersecting point.

7. Make a 3″ slit in the interfacing only.

8. Turn the petal shape right side out and gently push out the seams with the rounded end of a spatula. Press well.

Enclosing the Hexagons

1. Lay the petal shape right side down on the work surface. Center the embroidered hexagon, right side up, on the petal shape.

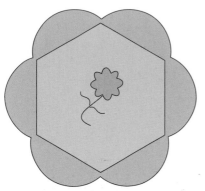

Center embellished hexagon.

2. Fold the petals onto the hexagon and glue in place with appliqué glue. Then press the panel well from the back with a warm iron.

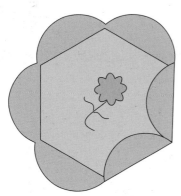

Fold flower petals onto hexagon.

3. Machine stitch with matching thread as close as possible to the edge of the petals.

Machine stitch.

4. Embroider around the petals with a crochet cotton yarn and a twisted chain stitch (page 93).

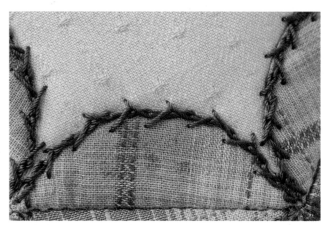

Stitch along folded edge.

Assembly

Use Pattern 15 (pullout page P4) for the layout plan.

1. Use a closely worked overcast or whip stitch and a neutral sewing thread to join the hexagons with right sides facing.

2. Gently turn the bag right side out.

3. Clip the handles in place.

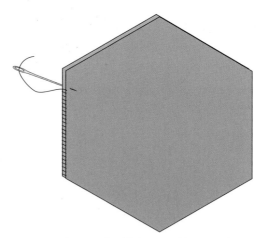

Sew together fabric-covered hexagon pieces.

Trinket Box

Finished size: 7″ × 3½″

Reminiscent of a Victorian trinket box, this project features all that is traditional crazy quilting.

FABRIC AND SUPPLIES

- Assorted fabrics at least 4½˝ × 6˝
- 1 piece of foundation fabric 6˝ × 9½˝
- 1 piece of lightweight fusible fleece 6˝ × 9½˝ (I use Vilene H630 by Pellon.)
- 1 piece of lining fabric 6˝ × 9½˝
- 1 piece of template plastic 3¾˝ × 7¼˝ for lid panel
- 3 pieces of outer fabric 6˝ × 9½˝
- 3 pieces of lightweight fusible fleece 6˝ × 9½˝ (I use Vilene H630 by Pellon.)
- 3 pieces of lining fabric 6˝ × 9½˝
- 3 pieces of template plastic 3¾˝ × 6¾˝ for front, back, and base panels
- 2 pieces of outer fabric 5½˝ × 5½˝
- 2 pieces of lightweight fusible fleece 5½˝ × 5½˝ (I use Vilene H630 by Pellon.)
- 2 pieces of lining fabric 5½˝ × 5½˝
- 2 pieces of template plastic 3¼˝ × 3¼˝ for side panels
- Craft glue

NEEDLES AND THREADS

- Milliners #03 needle for

  Perle cotton #8 thread
- Milliners #09 needle for

  Nymo beading thread
- Chenille #22 needle for

  2mm, 4mm, and 7mm silk ribbons

  Silk perle #8 thread

  Gold metallic thread

EMBELLISHMENTS

- Small flower sequins
- Seed beads
- Butterfly charm
- 7mm silk ribbon trim for the lid's edge
- 7mm silk ribbon
- Buttons

Threads, charms, beads, and fabrics

Construction

Pattern includes ¼˝ seam allowance.

Making the Lid

Use Pattern 16 (pullout page P3) for the lid and plastic insert.

1. Follow the foundation piecing method (page 10) to complete the lid panel.

2. Follow the stitch maps (pages 67–69) to complete the seam treatments.

3. Trim the completed lid panel on the cutting line.

Stitch Maps

LID PIECE 1

A. Stacked buttons (page 92)
• Perle cotton #8 thread

Note: Complete this section when Finishing the Lid, Step 7 (page 69).

LID SEAM TREATMENT A

A. Stab stitch (page 91)
- 4mm silk ribbon

B. Padded stab stitch (page 88)
- 7mm silk ribbon

C. Feather stitch (page 84)
- Perle cotton #8 thread

D. Ribbon stitch (page 89)
- 4mm silk ribbon

E. Knotted fly stitch (page 86)
- 4mm silk ribbon

F. Single-bead stitch (page 91)
- Nymo beading thread

LID SEAM TREATMENT B

A. Stab stitch (page 91)
- Silk perle #8 thread

B. Beaded/couched sequin (page 81)
- Nymo beading thread

LID SEAM TREATMENT C

A. Lazy daisy stitch (page 87)
- Silk perle #8 thread

B. Loop stitch and flower (page 88)
- 7mm silk ribbon

C. Twisted chain stitch (page 93)
- 2mm silk ribbon

LID SEAM TREATMENT D

A. Ruched silk ribbon garland (page 90)
- 7mm silk ribbon

B. Stab stitch (page 91)
- Silk perle #8 thread

LID PIECE 4

A. Charm (page 82)
  • Nymo beading thread

B. Stab stitch (page 91)
  • Gold metallic thread

C. Single-bead stitch (page 91)
  • Nymo beading thread

LID PIECE 5

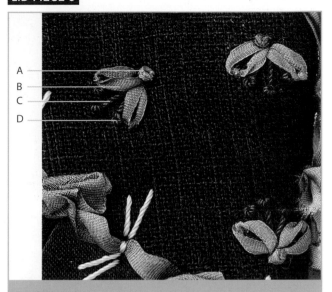

A. Colonial knot (page 82)
  • 2mm silk ribbon

B. Lazy daisy stitch (page 87)
  • 2mm silk ribbon

C. Stab stitch (page 91)
  • Silk perle #8 thread

D. Colonial knot (page 82)
  • Silk perle #8 thread

Finishing the Lid

1. Trace the perimeter line of the lid panel onto the wrong side of the lining fabric. Trim to the cutting line.

2. Place the lining fabric on the embellished lid panel, right sides facing. Stitch around the panel, keeping a short side open.

3. Trim the corners and turn the panel through to the right side.

Use Pattern 16 (pullout page P3) for the plastic insert.

4. Trace the plastic insert panel shape onto the template plastic. Cut on the newly marked line and trim the sharp corners.

5. Roll the template plastic lengthwise and insert it into the lid panel. Flatten the panel, pushing the seam allowance to the lining side. The fabric should fit tightly over the plastic.

6. Fold the raw edges in ¼″ and slipstitch the opening closed.

7. Add stacked buttons (page 92) to the center of the right side of the lid.

8. Use 7mm silk ribbon to add ruched silk ribbon garland (page 90) to the perimeter of the lid.

Making the Front, Back, Base, and Side Panels

Use Pattern 17 (pullout page P3) for the front, back, base, and plastic insert.

Use Pattern 18 (pullout page P3) for the side panels and plastic insert.

1. Follow the stitch map (below) to complete the embroidery.

2. Fuse the fleece to the wrong side of the front panel.

3. Trim the completed panel to the cutting line.

Stitch Map

A. Loop stitch and flower (page 88)
  • 7mm silk ribbon

B. Colonial knot (page 82)
  • 7mm silk ribbon

C. Twisted chain stitch (page 93)
  • 2mm silk ribbon

D. Lazy daisy stitch (page 87)
  • Silk perle #8 thread

Finishing the Front, Back, Base, and Side Panels

1. Trace the perimeter line of the front panel onto the wrong side of the lining fabric.

2. Trim to the cutting line.

3. Place the lining fabric on the embellished panel, right sides facing.

4. Machine stitch around the panel, leaving one side seam open.

5. Trim the corners and turn the panel through to the right side.

Use Pattern 17 (pullout page P3) for the plastic insert.

6. Trace the plastic insert panel shape onto the template plastic. Cut on the newly marked line and trim the sharp corners.

7. Roll the template plastic lengthwise and insert it into the panel. Flatten the panel, pushing the seam allowance to the lining side. The fabric should fit tightly over the plastic.

8. Fold the raw edges in ¼" and slipstitch the opening closed.

9. Repeat Steps 1–3 of Making the Front, Back, Base, and Side Panels and Steps 1–8 above for the back, base, and side panels.

Assembly

1. Place the wrong sides of the panels together. Join the panels with a beaded glove stitch (page 86), using perle cotton #8 thread and a milliners #03 needle. The working stitch is beaded with a seed bead.

2. Attach stacked buttons (page 92) at each corner and at the center of the underside of the box base.

3. Turn the box upside down and glove stitch the base in place in the same manner as the panels.

Sewing Basket

Finished size: 8″ × 5″

A few of my favorite things: vintage doilies, yo-yos, and sewing baskets.

FABRIC AND SUPPLIES

- Assorted fabric scraps at least 7˝ × 7˝
- 3 pieces of foundation fabric 7˝ × 7˝
- 3 pieces of embroidered doily at least 4˝ × 5˝
- 3 pieces of fabric 7˝ × 7˝ for doily panel
- 6 pieces of lining fabric 7˝ × 7˝
- 3 pieces of fusible web at least 4˝ × 5˝
- 6 pieces of lightweight fusible fleece 7˝ × 7 (I use Vilene H630 by Pellon.)˝
- 2 pieces of lining fabric 8˝ × 8˝ for base
- 1 piece of lightweight fusible fleece 8˝ × 8˝ for base (I use Vilene H630 by Pellon.)
- 1 piece of poly boning ½˝ × 17˝
- 1 piece of fabric 1¾˝ × 17˝ for handle
- 20 fabric circles 3˝ × 3˝ for yo-yos
- 1 small Clover yo-yo maker (optional)
- 1 sheet of template plastic 12½˝ × 18½˝

NEEDLES AND THREADS

- Milliners #03 needle for

  Perle cotton #8 and #12 thread
- Milliners #09 needle for

  Nymo beading thread
- Chenille #22 needle for

  2 mm, 4mm, and 7 mm silk ribbon

  7mm organza ribbon

  Tulle ribbon

  Gold metallic thread

EMBELLISHMENTS

- Small flower sequins
- Seed beads
- Pearl seed beads
- Heart-shaped bead for spider body
- Rice pearl for butterfly body
- 2 butterfly-shaped beads

Fabrics, doily, ribbon, and threads

Construction

Pattern includes ¼˝ seam allowance.

Making the Crazy Panels

Use Pattern 19 (pullout page P2) for the crazy panels.

1. Follow the foundation piecing method (page 10) to complete the 3 crazy panels.

2. Follow the stitch maps (pages 73–75) to complete the seam treatments.

3. Trim the completed front panels to the cutting line.

Stitch Maps

Crazy Panel A

SEAM TREATMENT A

A. Beaded/couched sequin (page 81)
- Nymo beading thread

B. Stab stitch (page 91)
- Perle cotton #12 thread

C. Lazy daisy stitch (page 87)
- 2mm silk ribbon

D. Stem stitch with beads (page 93)
- Perle cotton #8 thread

SEAM TREATMENT B

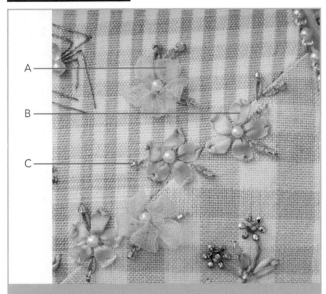

A. Loop stitch and flower (page 88)
- 7mm organza ribbon

B. Ribbon stitch flower (page 89)
- 4mm silk ribbon

C. Lazy daisy stitch with bead (page 87)
- Perle cotton #8 thread

PIECE 1

A. Spider (page 91)

See stitch dictionary for threads.

Crazy Panel B

SEAM TREATMENT B

A. Loop stitch and flower (page 88)
- 4mm silk ribbon

B. Stab stitch (page 91)
- Perle cotton #12 thread

C. Beaded leaf (page 80)
- Nymo beading thread

SEAM TREATMENT A

A. Padded stab stitch (page 88)
- 4mm silk ribbon

B. Beaded/couched sequin (page 81)
- Nymo beading thread

C. Stem stitch (page 92)
- Perle cotton #8 thread

D. Stab stitch (page 91)
- Perle cotton #12 thread

PIECE 1

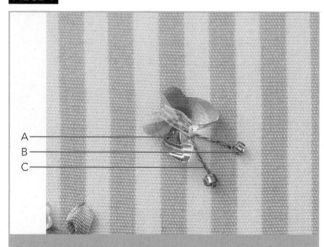

A. Single-bead stitch (page 91)
- Nymo beading thread

B. Single-bead stitch (page 91)
- Nymo beading thread

C. Stab stitch (page 91)
- Gold metallic thread

Crazy Panel C

A. Lazy daisy stitch (page 87)
• 4mm silk ribbon

B. Spiderweb rose (page 91)
• 7mm silk ribbon

C. Loop stitch (page 88)
• Tulle ribbon

D. Beaded forget-me-not (page 80)
• Nymo beading thread

E. Ruched rose (page 90)
• 7mm silk ribbon

SEAM TREATMENT A

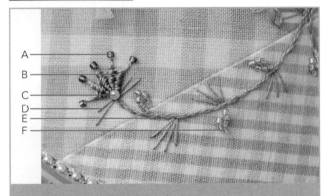

A. Single-bead stitch (page 91)
• Nymo beading thread

B. Woven spiderweb (page 94)
• Perle cotton #8 thread

C. Single-bead stitch (page 91)
• Nymo beading thread

D. Stab stitch (page 91)
• Perle cotton #12 thread

E. Stem stitch (page 92)
• Perle cotton #8 thread

F. Beaded leaf (page 80)
• Nymo beading thread

PIECE 1

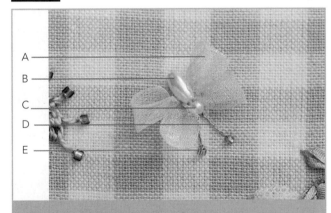

A. Loop stitch (page 88)
• 7mm organza ribbon

B. Single-bead stitch (page 91)
• Nymo beading thread

C. Single-bead stitch (page 91)
• Nymo beading thread

D. Stab stitch (page 91)
• Gold metallic thread

E. Single-bead stitch (page 91)
• Nymo beading thread

Finishing the Crazy Panels

Use Pattern 19 (pullout page P2) for the crazy panel linings and plastic inserts.

1. Trace the crazy panel onto the wrong side of the lining fabric. Trim to the cutting line.

2. Place the lining fabric on the embellished panel, right sides facing.

3. Machine stitch around the panel, leaving the bottom seam open.

4. Trim the corners and turn the panel through to the right side.

5. Trace the plastic insert panel shape onto the template plastic. Cut on the newly marked line and trim the sharp corners.

6. Roll the template plastic lengthwise and insert it into the side panel. Flatten the panel, pushing the seam allowance to the lining side. The fabric should fit tightly over the plastic.

7. Fold the raw edges under ¼″ and slipstitch the opening closed.

8. Repeat Steps 1–7 for the remaining 2 panels.

Making the Doily Panels

Use Pattern 20 (pullout page P2) for the doily panel.

1. Trace the doily panel shape onto the wrong side of the fabric.

2. Apply fusible web to the back of the doily, following the manufacturer's instructions. Cut the doily to the desired shape. Fuse the doily onto the panel fabric.

3. Fuse the fleece to the wrong side of the panel. Trim to the cutting line.

4. Follow the stitch maps (at right and page 77) to complete the panel, using seam treatments A or B.

Stitch Maps

Doily Panel A

SEAM TREATMENT A

A. Feather stitch (page 84)
- 4mm silk ribbon

B. Beaded/couched sequin (page 81)
- Nymo beading thread

Doily Panel B

Doily Panel C

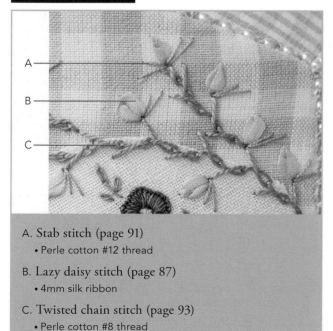

A. Stab stitch (page 91)
  • Perle cotton #12 thread

B. Lazy daisy stitch (page 87)
  • 4mm silk ribbon

C. Twisted chain stitch (page 93)
  • Perle cotton #8 thread

Finishing the Doily Panels

Use Pattern 20 (pullout page P2) for the doily panel linings and plastic inserts.

1. Trace the doily panel onto the wrong side of the lining fabric.

2. Place the lining fabric on the embellished panel, right sides facing.

3. Machine stitch around the panel, leaving the bottom seam open.

4. Trim the corners and turn the panel through to the right side.

5. Trace the plastic insert panel shape onto the template plastic. Cut on the marked line and trim the sharp corners.

6. Roll the template plastic lengthwise and insert it into the side panel. Flatten the panel, pushing the seam allowance to the lining side. The fabric should fit tightly over the plastic.

7. Fold the raw edges in ¼" and slipstitch the opening closed.

8. Repeat Steps 1–7 for the 2 remaining doily panels.

Preparing the Hexagon Base

Use Pattern 21 (pullout page P2) for the hexagon base and plastic insert.

1. Trace the base pattern onto the wrong sides of both pieces of base fabrics.

2. Fuse the fleece to the wrong side of a piece of base fabric.

3. Trim both base fabric pieces to the cutting line.

4. Stitch around the base, right sides facing, leaving a side open.

5. Trim the corners and turn the panel through to the right side.

6. Trace the plastic insert onto the template plastic. Cut on the marked line and trim the sharp corners.

7. Roll the template plastic lengthwise and insert it into the side panel. Flatten the panel, pushing the seam allowance to the lining side. The fabric should fit tightly over the plastic.

8. Fold the raw edges in ¼″ and slipstitch the opening closed.

Preparing the Handles

1. Fold a piece of the 1¾″ × 17″ fabric in half lengthwise, right sides facing.

2. Stitch the long sides using a scant ¼″ seam.

3. Turn the piece right side out.

4. Press well, making sure the seam is centered on the wrong side of the handle.

5. Stitch as close as possible to the edge of both long sides of the handle fabric.

6. Insert the poly boning.

Assembly

1. Make 18 yo-yos (see Hexagon Purse, Making the Yo-Yos, page 48, or follow the manufacturer's instructions on the yo-yo maker).

2. Fold the yo-yos in half and slipstitch in place, enclosing the top edge of each panel. There should be 3 yo-yos to each panel.

3. Alternate a crazy panel and a doily panel. With the wrong sides of the panels facing each other, join them with a beaded glove stitch (page 86), using perle cotton #8 thread and a milliners #03 needle. The traveling stitch is beaded with a pearl bead; the working stitch is beaded with a seed bead.

4. Turn the basket upside down and glove stitch the base using the beaded glove technique.

5. Slipstitch the handles in place on opposite sides of the sewing bucket.

6. Make 2 more yo-yos.

7. Cover the raw edges and the stitching of the handles with a yo-yo.

Stitch Dictionary

Basic Embroidery

Assortment of embroidery threads

Don't make your stitches too tight or the detail will disappear into the fabric layers, but do try to make your stitches even! Crazy quilting is worked on a foundation fabric, so a small knot to begin and end your stitches is perfectly acceptable.

Silk Ribbon Embroidery

Assortment of silk ribbons

Threading the Needle and Knotting the Thread

A chenille needle is used in all silk ribbon embroidery.

THREADING THE NEEDLE

1. Cut a 10″–12″ length of ribbon.

2. Thread an end of the ribbon through the eye of the needle.

3. Turn the point of the needle and pierce the threaded end of the ribbon.

4. Hold the point of the needle as you pull down the long end of the ribbon, allowing the ribbon to "lock" over the eye.

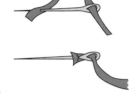

KNOTTING THE RIBBON

1. Make a ¼″ fold at the end of the ribbon.

2. Pierce the fold with the point of the needle.

3. Pull the ribbon down over the needle to form a soft knot at the end.

FASTENING OFF

1. Use the blunt end of the needle to pass the ribbon under the back of a previously worked stitch.

2. Form a loop with the ribbon and pass the needle through the loop.

3. Gently pull the ribbon until the knot is tight.

Tips

- It is very important to keep the ribbon on the back of your work untwisted. This will allow the ribbon to fan out on the surface of your work.

- Work with a loose tension when embroidering with silk ribbon.

Beading

Beading needles and threads

NOTES

- It is important to use a strong beading thread, such as Nymo or Silamide thread.

- It is advisable to use a hoop while beading.

- Begin and end beading securely with anchoring knots.

- Match your thread to the bead and not to the fabric.

- Always insert your needle into the fabric at 90° and not at an angle.

- Knot before and after every bead or sequin.

- To prevent fabric puckering under the beads, do not have your traveling thread longer than 1″.

Tip Do not bead within ½″ of the project's perimeter. Tack the beads that are needed to complete the seam treatments on the muslin for safekeeping.

Beaded Forget-Me-Not

The forget-me-not flower is made and then couched onto the surface of the work.

1. Thread a beading needle with approximately 12″ of Nymo beading thread. Pick up 5 or 6 pearl or round beads.

2. Pass the needle through the first 3 beads to form a circle with the thread.

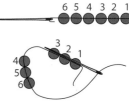

To finish with a center bead, continue to Step 3. To finish with a colonial knot, skip to Step 6.

3. Pick up a bead of a different color.

4. Pass the needle through the sixth pearl bead.

5. Pull both threads firmly so the center bead sits in the middle of the pearl beads.

6. Knot the threads tightly.

7. Use a thread to couch the flower to the surface of the work.

Couching

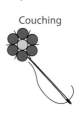

8. Pass the remaining thread to the back of the work and form an anchoring knot.

9. Make a colonial knot (page 82) using ribbon if no bead was added.

Beaded Leaf

1. Bring the needle to the surface of the work at A and pick up 3 beads.

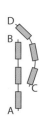

2. Reinsert the needle at B.

3. Bring the needle to the surface at C and pick up 3 beads.

4. Reinsert the needle at D, allowing the last 3 beads to form a gentle curve.

5. Finish with an anchoring knot.

Beaded/Couched Sequin

1. Bring the needle to the surface of the work and pick up a sequin and seed bead.

2. Hold the seed bead between the thumb and index finger and reinsert the needle through the sequin. The seed bead will now hold the sequin in place.

3. Finish with an anchoring knot on the wrong side of the fabric under the sequin before traveling along to the next sequin.

Alternative, a sequin *without a bead* can simply be couched down with a matching Nymo beading thread.

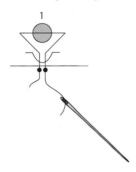

Bullion Knot

1. Bring the needle to the surface of the work at A.

2. Reinsert at B (the distance between A and B will be the length of the bullion knot).

3. Emerge at A but do not pull the needle all the way through the fabric.

4. Wrap the working thread around the needle as many times as is required to equal the size of the backstitch.

5. Support the wraps on the needle with the thumb and index finger and pull the needle through. Pull the thread away from and then toward you.

6. With the wraps evenly packed on the thread, reinsert the needle at B to end the bullion knot.

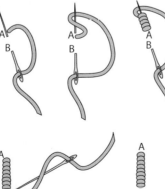

Bullion Lazy Daisy Stitch

1. Bring the needle to the surface of the work at A.

2. Make a loop with the thread/ribbon. Reinsert the needle at A and emerge at B, inside the loop.

3. Hold the loop down with the nonworking and wrap the thread/ribbon around the needles as many times as desired.

4. Support the wraps on the needle and pull the needle through.

5. Reinsert the needle at the tip of the bullion to anchor the stitch.

Buttonhole Wing Stitch

1. Make a small lazy daisy stitch (page 87).

2. Reinsert the needle at A and make another lazy daisy stitch slightly larger than the first one.

3. Repeat Step 2 to make a second lazy daisy stitch larger than the previous one.

4. Finish with a small anchoring stitch.

Button

Use thread or ribbon to attach buttons to the work.

Chain Stitch

1. Bring the needle to the surface of the work at A.

2. Loop the thread and reinsert the needle at B.

3. Emerge a short distance away at C and, with the thread under the needle, pull through.

4. Loop the thread and insert the needle exactly where the thread emerged in the previous loop.

5. Continue as desired, finishing with a small stitch over the last loop.

Chain Stitch Rose

Begin in the center and work in a circular motion with small chain stitches (page 82) that progressively get larger to create the desired size.

Charm

1. Choose a Nymo beading thread that will blend with the charm and the fabric to which it is being attached.

2. Sew on the charm, making the thread as invisible as possible.

Chevron Stitch

1. Bring the needle to the surface of the work at A and then insert the needle at B; exit a half-stitch length to the left at C.

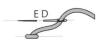

2. Insert the needle at D and exit a half-stitch length to the left at E.

3. Insert the needle a stitch length to the right at F and exit a half-stitch length to the left at D.

4. Continue as desired.

Chevron Stitch with Beads

Follow the chevron stitch instructions (above), adding beads on the horizontal lines of the chevron stitch.

Colonial Knot

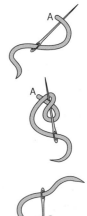

1. Bring the thread to the surface of the work at A.

2. Cross the thread/ribbon over the needle from left to right. Wrap the thread/ribbon under the needle and then around the needle from right to left (creating a figure 8 on your needle).

3. Reinsert the needle at B, close to where it originally emerged.

4. Hold the needle in place and gently pull the working thread/ribbon taut toward the surface of the work. A firm knot will form.

5. Pull the needle through to the back of the work.

Coral Stitch

1. Work from right to left to bring the thread/ribbon to the surface of the work at A.

2. Lay the thread/ribbon along the design line.

3. Secure the thread/ribbon with the left thumb of the nonworking hand.

4. Loop the thread/ribbon to the right and take a small stitch under the thread/ribbon from B to C.

5. With the thread/ribbon under the needle, pull through.

6. Continue as desired.

7. To finish, stitch the thread/ribbon down on the wrong side of the work. The segments of thread/ribbon between the knots may be smooth or raised, and the line can zigzag, pivoting at each point. Keep the tension loose.

Cretan Stitch

1. Bring the needle to the surface of the work at A.

2. Loop the working thread/ribbon to the right and reinsert at B.

3. With the thread/ribbon under the needle, emerge at C.

4. Loop the thread/ribbon to the right and reinsert at D.

5. With the thread/ribbon under the needle, emerge at E.

6. Continue as required.

Delphinium

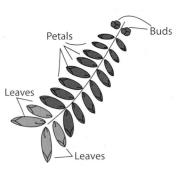

Stem:

Stem stitch (page 92)

Perle cotton #8 thread

Milliners #03 needle

Leaves:

Ribbon stitch (page 89)
or lazy daisy stitch (page 87)

Silk ribbon of choice

Chenille #22 needle

Petals:

Ribbon stitch (page 89)

4mm silk ribbon

Chenille #22 needle

Buds:

Colonial knot (page 82)

4mm silk ribbon

Chenille #22 needle

Feather Stitch

1. Bring the needle to the surface of the work at A.

2. Loop the thread/ribbon to the left and insert at B (in line with A).

3. With the thread/ribbon under the needle, emerge at C (between A and B), forming a V shape.

4. Insert the needle at D, in line with C. Loop the thread/ribbon to the right and emerge at E.

5. Continue as desired, alternating the stitches from left to right. Finish with a small stitch over the last loop.

Feather Stitch with Beads

Follow the feather stitch instructions (above) and pick up the desired amount of beads at Step 1.

Fern Stitch

1. Bring the needle to the surface of the work at A.

2. Reinsert at B and reemerge at A.

3. Insert at C and reemerge at A to complete the left-hand stitch.

4. Insert the needle at D and emerge at E to complete the right-hand stitch and set up for the next group.

The 3 stitches that make up a fern stitch are usually the same length.

Fishbone Stitch

1. Use an erasable pencil to draw a small leaf shape with a line down the center.

2. Beginning at the flower's tip, make a small stab stitch (page 91) from A to B, ensuring that the ribbon is not twisted.

3. Emerge at C, reinsert at D, and emerge at E. Insert again at F and emerge at G.

4. Continue until the leaf shape is filled.

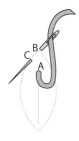  

Five-Petal Flower

1. Cut a 6″ length of 7mm ribbon.

2. Use an erasable pen to mark out the ribbon into 5 equal areas.

3. Using a matching sewing thread, begin at an end and stitch as shown. *Note: The thread loops over the ribbon edge.*

4. Once stitching is complete, gently pull the thread to gather the ribbon into 5 petals along the thread.

5. Manipulate the petals so they are flat and untwisted.

6. Secure the last petal with a few stitches to prevent unraveling.

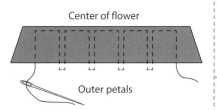

Center of flower

Outer petals

7. Stitch the flower in place.

Fly Stitch

1. Bring the needle to the surface of the work at A.

2. Insert at B and, with the thread/ribbon under the needle, emerge at C.

3. Reinsert at D to form the anchor stitch.

The extended fly stitch has a longer anchoring stitch.

Fly Stitch with Beads

1. Follow the fly stitch instructions (at left) but with the following changes:

2. Pick up 4 beads at Step 1.

3. Divide the beads to leave a pair on either side of C.

4. Reinsert the needle at D to form the anchor stitch.

Fly Stitch Leaf

1. Draw a small leaf shape on the fabric.

2. The leaf is made up of a series of fly stitches (at left) that progressively get larger to suit the leaf's shape. The first fly stitch is made at the tip of the leaf shape.

3. To complete the leaf, make a small stab stitch (page 91) in the middle of the first fly stitch.

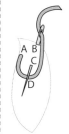

Free-Form Flower with Beaded Center

Silk ribbon of choice and Nymo beading thread

Milliners #10 needle

1. Thread the needle with a Nymo beading thread to match the ribbon.

2. Make a knot at the end of the thread.

3. Starting at an end of the ribbon, make small running stitches along the bottom edge.

4. Gather the ribbon to form a flower.

5. Stitch several times over the base of the flower so it can't pull out.

6. Stitch the flower to the desired seam.

7. Use a single bead stitch (page 91) to add beads at the flower's center.

Herringbone Stitch

1. Bring the needle to the surface of the work at A.

2. Insert at B.

3. Emerge at C (to the left of B).

4. Reinsert at D (to the right of B).

5. Emerge at E (to the left of D).

6. Continue as desired.

I like to make a small, horizontal couching stitch where the 2 threads cross.

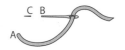

Glove Stitch

1. Place the pieces of fabric together following the project instructions.

2. Bring the needle to the surface of the work at A.

3. Wrap the stitch over the top of the fabric edge and emerge at A, forming a straight vertical stitch. This is the "working" stitch; the thread tension should be taut.

4. Make a diagonal "traveling" stitch over the fabric edge, emerging at B.

5. Continue as required. End with a small anchoring stitch.

As required, the glove stitch can include a bead on the "working" stitch or the "traveling" stitch.

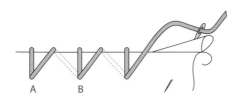

Knotted Fly Stitch

1. Bring the needle to the surface of the work at A.

2. Insert at B and then, with the thread/ribbon under the needle, emerge at C.

3. Without going through the fabric, pass the thread under the fly stitch at C and over the looped working thread. Pull snug to form a knot.

4. Reinsert at D to form the anchor stitch.

The extended fly stitch has a longer anchoring stitch.

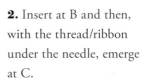

Lazy Daisy Stitch

1. Bring the needle to the surface of the work at A.

2. Make a loop with the thread/ribbon.

3. Hold the loop down with the nonworking hand and reinsert the needle at B, near to where it first emerged.

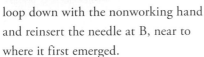

4. With the thread/ribbon under the needle, make a small stitch from B to C to anchor the loop.

5. Finish with a small stab stitch at D.

Lazy Daisy Stitch with Bead

1. Follow Steps 1–3 of the lazy daisy stitch instructions (above).

2. Pick up the desired number of beads on the needle and then complete Step 4 of the lazy daisy stitch instructions.

Lazy Daisy Stitch Flower

1. Use an erasable pencil to mark a small circle on the fabric where the flower center will be.

2. Make a series of lazy daisy stitches (above) around the outside of the marked circle.

3. Work in a clockwise direction, keeping the back of the circle clear of any silk ribbon and the tension of the lazy daisy stitches relaxed.

4. Add colonial knots (page 82) or beads to the center.

Looped Bullion Knot Stitch

1. Bring the needle to the surface of the work at A.

2. Reinsert at B, as close to A as possible.

3. Emerge at A, but do not pull the needle all the way through the fabric.

4. Wrap the working thread around the needle as many times as required, creating a loop.

5. Support the wraps on the needle with the thumb and index finger and pull the needle through. Pull the thread away from and then toward you.

6. With the wraps evenly packed on the thread, reinsert the needle at C to end the looped bullion knot stitch.

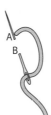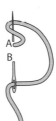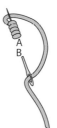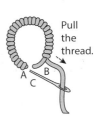

Pull the thread.

Looped Ribbon Stitch

1. Bring the ribbon to the surface of the work at A.

2. Lay the ribbon flat. Allowing enough ribbon to form a loop, insert the needle through the ribbon as close to A as possible.

3. Pull the ribbon gently through the work at B. The ribbon will curl inward to form a loop (be careful not to pull too tightly).

4. Secure the ribbon on the wrong side of the work to end.

Loop Stitch and Flower

1. Bring the ribbon to the surface of the work at A.

2. Make a tiny back stitch and reinsert at B.

3. Place a pencil or straw through the ribbon loop. Keeping the ribbon untwisted, gently pull the ribbon through over the pencil. Remove the pencil once the ribbon is taut.

4. Repeat Steps 1–3 for the next loop stitch. Secure the ribbon on the wrong side of the work to end.

To make a loop stitch flower:

1. Mark a small circle with an erasable pencil where the flower center will be.

2. Make a series of looped stitch petals around the outside of the marked circle. Work in a clockwise direction, because it is important to keep the back of the marked circle clear of any silk ribbon.

3. Add colonial knots (page 82) or beads to the center of the flower.

Palestrina Knot Stitch

1. Working horizontally, bring the needle to the surface of the fabric at A, reinsert at B, and emerge at C.

2. Without going through the fabric, pass the needle under the straight stitch between A and B and pull through gently, keeping the stitch loose.

3. Pass the needle under the straight stitch between A and B, keeping the previous stitch and the looped thread or ribbon under the needle. Pull through.

4. Continue as desired, spacing the knots by taking another small stitch at D and E to repeat.

Padded Stab Stitch

1. Bring the ribbon to the surface of the work and make a colonial knot (page 82).

2. Form a stab stitch (page 91) over the colonial knot, keeping the tension of the stab stitch relaxed.

3. Secure the ribbon on the wrong side of the work to end.

Plume Stitch

1. Work this stitch toward you; begin where you would like the plume stitch to end.

2. Use an erasable pen to mark the fabric with a temporary guideline.

3. Bring the needle to the surface of the work at A and form a small loop by inserting the needle at B, a small distance from where it emerged.

4. Emerge through the base of the previous loop at C. Keep the ribbon untwisted as you work the series of loops.

5. Stitch the ribbon down on the wrong side of the work to end.

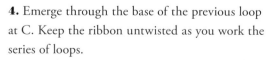

Raised Chain Stitch

Perle cotton #8 thread

Milliners #03 needle

Silk ribbon of choice

Chenille #22 needle

1. Use perle cotton #8 thread to make a ladder of small stitches ¼" apart, with the width no wider than the silk ribbon used.

2. Change to the silk ribbon.

3. Bring the needle to the surface of the fabric center above the top rung.

4. Without going through the fabric and keeping the thread/ribbon to the right, pass the thread under the top stitch and pull through gently, keeping the stitch loose.

5. Keep the thread/ribbon under the needle and pass the needle under the top stitch again from the top.

6. Pull the thread through to form a knot, keeping the tension of the thread/ribbon loose.

7. Continue along the ladder stitches, going up on the left and down on the right on every stitch.

8. Insert the needle to the back of the work and fasten off.

Ribbon Stitch

1. Bring the ribbon to the surface of the work at A.

2. Lay the ribbon flat and insert the needle through the ribbon where you want the tip of the stitch to be.

3. Pull the ribbon gently through the work. The ribbon will curl inward to form a point (be careful not to pull too tightly).

4. Secure the ribbon on the wrong side of the work to end.

Ribbon Stitch Flower

1. Use an erasable pencil to mark a small circle where the flower center will be.

2. Make a series of ribbon stitches (above) around the outside of the small marked circle as petals. Work in a clockwise direction, since it is very important to keep the back of the marked circle clear of any silk ribbon.

3. Add colonial knots (page 82) or seed beads for the center of the flower.

Keep the tension of the ribbon stitches relaxed and untwisted.

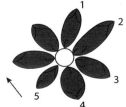

Ruched Rose

1. Bring the ribbon to the surface of the work at A.

2. Hold the ribbon in the nonworking hand approximately 3″ away from the surface of the work. Form a colonial knot (page 82).

3. Keeping the knot on the needle, form small gathering stitches along the length of the ribbon.

4. Once you reach the end of the ribbon, reinsert the needle into the work at B.

5. Gently pull the ribbon through. A small rose will form.

6. Secure the ribbon on the wrong side of the work to end.

Tip A variegated silk ribbon will give your rose shading without your having to change the ribbon during stitching.

Ruched Silk Ribbon Garland

Silk ribbon of choice

Embroidery thread

Chenille #22 needle

Milliners #10 needle

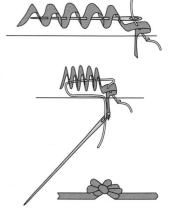

1. Thread a milliners needle with a single strand of embroidery thread to match the silk ribbon.

2. Bring the ribbon to the surface of the work.

3. Bring the embroidery thread to the surface of the work a short distance from where the ribbon first emerged.

4. Use the embroidery thread to form a number of small gathering stitches along the ribbon. The last gathering stitch should end with the thread on the underside of the ribbon.

5. Reinsert the embroidery thread into the work alongside where it emerged.

6. Gently pull the thread through the work; a small rose will form on the surface of the work.

7. Form an anchoring knot on the wrong side of the work.

8. Continue as desired; don't bring the ribbon to the back between the roses. Reinsert the ribbon and secure on the wrong side of the work to end.

These garlands may be formed into geometric shapes, zigzags, or gentle folds.

Single-Bead Button

1. Come to the surface of the button through a buttonhole.

2. Pick up a single bead large enough to cover the hole.

3. Reinsert the needle into the same hole. Secure with an anchoring knot.

4. Repeat Steps 1–3 for the adjacent hole.

Single-Bead Stitch

Bead of choice

Nymo beading thread

Milliners #10 needle

1. When attaching a single bead of any size, bring the thread from the back to the front.

2. Put the bead on the needle and reinsert the needle into the fabric to the back of the work. Form an anchoring knot.

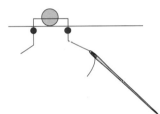

Spider

Head and body:

Single-bead stitch (above)

Nymo beading thread

Legs:

Stab stitch (at right)

Gold metallic thread

Chenille #22 needle

NOTE
Remember that spiders have eight very long legs.

Spiderweb Rose

1. With an erasable pencil, mark a temporary circle with 5 evenly spaced spokes.

2. With a single strand of coordinating thread, make a fly stitch (page 85) to create the first 3 spokes and then a stab stitch (below) for the other 2 spokes.

3. Bring the ribbon to the surface of the work at the center of the spokes.

4. Without piercing the fabric or ribbon, weave the ribbon over and under the spokes, allowing the ribbon to twist. Keep the weaving soft and loose.

5. Continue until the rose is full. Reinsert the needle to make the final petal.

6. Secure the ribbon on the back of the work to end.

7. Add seed beads or colonial knots (page 82) for the rose centers.

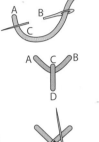

Stab Stitch

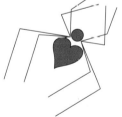

Bring the needle to the surface of the work at A and work a stitch to B at the required length and direction.

Do not make stab stitches too long, because they tend to catch.

Twisted thread is best for this stitch. When using silk ribbon, twist slightly between A and B.

Stab Stitch Couching

Silk ribbon or thread of choice

Chenille #22 needle or milliners #10 needle

1. Lay the 7mm silk ribbon on the desired seam.

2. Using 4mm silk ribbon, stab stitch (page 91) over the 7mm ribbon. Allow the ribbon to fan out between the couching stitches.

This technique may also be used on other forms of trim such as rayon tape, and couching stitches can be made with other threads.

Stab Stitch Leaf

The leaf is made up of a series of stab stitches (page 91) that progressively get smaller on each side of a central stitch.

To preserve the integrity of the thread, it is advisable to bring the needle from the perimeter of the leaf into a central point 0.

Stacked Buttons

Lay a button on top of another to create texture and color. Add beads as desired and stitch in place.

Stem Stitch

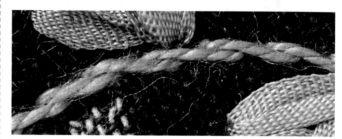

This stitch works from left to right as you keep the thread or ribbon below the needle.

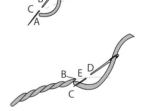

1. Bring the needle to the surface of the work at A. Reinsert at B.

2. Emerge at C (halfway between A and B).

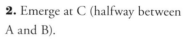

3. Reinsert at D and emerge beside B above the line of stitching.

4. Continue as desired.

Stem Stitch with Beads

To add texture to a stem stitch (page 92), simply pick up a bead on every second stitch.

Tufted Bud

1. Separate 12 strands of stranded cotton before threading the needle.

2. Bring the needle to the surface of the work from front to back.

3. Turn to the back of the work and complete a small holding stitch in the backing fabric.

4. Turn to the front of the work and bring the needle to the surface, very close to where the needle went down.

5. Hold all the strands firmly together and cut them to the desired length to form the tuft.

6. Form 2 overlapping stab stitches using 4mm silk ribbon at the base of the tufted bud.

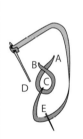

Holding stitch

Cut.

Twisted Chain Stitch

1. Bring the needle to the surface of the work at A.

2. Loop the thread to the right and reinsert at B.

3. With the thread under the needle, emerge at C (under A).

4. Loop the tread to the left and reinsert at D.

5. With the thread under the needle, emerge at E.

6. Loop the thread to the right and reinsert at F.

7. With the thread under the needle, emerge at C.

8. Repeat for the desired length, alternating the stitch form left to right.

9. Finish with a small stitch over the last chain.

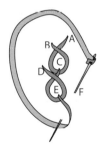

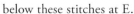

Wheatear Stitch

1. Work 2 stab stitches (page 91) at A and B, and then at C and B.

2. Bring the thread through below these stitches at E.

3. Pass the needle under the 2 stab stitches without entering the fabric.

4. Reinsert the needle at F.

5. Emerge at G to begin the next series of stitches.

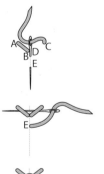

Whipped Chain Stitch

1. Work a foundation row of chain stitches (page 82).

2. Bring the thread to the surface at the start of the foundation chain.

3. Without piercing the fabric or chain stitch, keep the needle on the surface of the work and pass the thread over and under each link of the chain. Keep the tension relaxed and untwisted.

4. Reinsert the needle at the end of the last chain stitch and secure to end.

Woven Spiderweb

1. With an erasable pencil, draw a circle the size you want the finished web. Use a stab stitch (page 91) to make 8 evenly spaced spokes from A to B, C to D, E to F, and G to H.

2. Bring the needle to the surface of the work in the center of 2 spokes, and stab stitch across the center of the spokes.

3. Bring the needle to the surface of the work, near the center and between the 2 stitches. Without piercing the fabric, go over the spoke to the right and then under it, and then under the next spoke to the left.

4. Pull your thread toward the center.

5. Go back over the spoke you just went under, and then under it, and under the next spoke to the left.

6. Continue working counter-clockwise until the desired fullness has been reached. You are wrapping the thread around each spoke as you go.

7. Finish with a small anchoring stitch on the wrong side of the work. A partial spider web can also be worked over 5 stab stitches.

Woven Trellis Stitch

1. Follow the instructions for the stab stitch leaf (page 92) to complete 3 stab stitches.

2. Bring the needle to the surface of the work at the base of the leaf.

3. Weave the thread by taking the needle under the first and last stab stitches.

4. Turn and take the needle under the middle thread.

5. Repeat to fill the length of the stab stitches.

6. Insert the needle to the back of the work and fasten off.

Zigzag Chain Stitch

This stitch is worked in the same way as the chain stitch (page 82), except that you split the thread of the first chain link when you start the second link.

1. Angle the first link to the left and the second to the right.

2. Continue as desired.

About the Author

Photo by Ainslie Clouston

The Clouston family made Australia their home after emigrating from South Africa in 2002. Jenny has been an avid quilter, both sane and crazy, since the birth of her first child. Jenny's children, Gareth and Ainslie, have flown the nest, but she keeps herself busy writing and teaching crazy quilting. It was during the process of her first book, *Foolproof Crazy Quilting*, that Jenny discovered that she and her husband make quite a book-writing team. Jenny's creative spirit and Vaughn's meticulous attention to detail have proven to be a recipe for success.

ALSO BY JENNIFER CLOUSTON: